Altar Call

Inviting Response to the Gospel

Donna Schaper

Abingdon Press
Nashville

ALTAR CALL: INVITING RESPONSE TO THE GOSPEL

This book is printed on acid-free paper.

Library of Congress Cataloging-in-Publication Data

Schaper, Donna.
  Altar call: inviting response to the Gospel / Donna Schaper.
    p. cm.
  Includes bibliographical references.
  ISBN 0-687-09142-X (alk. paper)
  1. Evangelistic invitations.   I. Title.

BV3793 .S34 2001
269—dc21
                                            00-052206

Scripture quotations, unless otherwise indicated, are from the *New Revised Standard Version of the Bible,* copyright 1989, Division of Christian Education of the National Council of the Churches of Christ in the United States of America. Used by permission. All rights reserved.

01 02 03 04 05 06 07 08 09 10—10 9 8 7 6 5 4 3 2 1

MANUFACTURED IN THE UNITED STATES OF AMERICA

Contents

◆ ◆

Introduction   7

Chapter 1: Salvation as a Response to the Holy   21

Chapter 2: Money as a Call from and to the Altar   31

Chapter 3: Sharing Faith in a World of Holy Discontents   41

Chapter 4: The Importance of Small Groups   49

Chapter 5: The Matter of the Meeting   55

Chapter 6: The Matter of Time   63

Chapter 7: The Confidence of Knowing the Basics of Our Faith   75

Chapter 8: The Matter of Mission   91

Chapter 9: The Matter of Conversion   101

Chapter 10: The Call to Hospitality   111

Notes   119

Resources and References   121

Introduction

♦ ♦

"Evangelism is one beggar telling another where to find bread."
—D. T. Niles

Mainstream churches are made nervous by altar calls or responses to the call of God. We are not sure about the virtue of growth. We are afraid of sharing our faith. We are less convicted by our faith, due to many victories of so-called scientific thought among us. And finally, we are afraid to offend one another. Our code of politeness keeps certain matters private: religion joins sex in being a private matter. We are not supposed to talk about these things, so we do not.

Even when full of the gospel, we fear abusing it by sharing it openly or by responding to it. In this book, I talk of ways we might respond to the word of God, without offending our code of privacy too much. Some offense is inevitable and necessary—but inviting people to move too far outside their own experience in one step is simply naive. Mainstream people will move toward more responsiveness to the gospel if we give them multiple steps.

We dare not confuse the invitation to living the gospel life with an "ask" in terms of business or sales. They are structurally similar—in that we call forth a response or a buy-in—but, in application, they are also worlds apart. We are not selling the gospel. We are offering a gift.

The altar calls offered here are steps; they are an instruction in the art of gift giving. Our liturgies are oddly unbalanced. We hear the word of God, but we do not do it. We hear the call of God, but we do not return the phone call. We are more talk than action. It is like a dance that occurs all on one foot: here we learn some steps to respond to the rhythm of God's word—which exists in our hearts, privately. If we had more steplike altar calls, they would help stewardship campaigns as well as church attendance (not to mention faithfulness) by adding the "ask," or invitation, to our persuasions on behalf of our faith.

Major change in the privatized pattern of response to God's word is unlikely, but modest change is not. In this work, I want to outline simple ways that a moved heart could be translated to action in mainstream churches without becoming evangelical or Pentecostal or invasive of privacy, as these patterns are unfortunately confused with each other.

First, we need to critically analyze what we get from private faith. Mainstream Christians love critical analysis; we will not get very far with them if we do not have arguments ready for their defenses of the status quo. Why is the "ask" so automatic in business or sales but not in church? What is it about our product that we are protecting? What do we get from privacy about God, and what do we relinquish by enforcing patterns of spiritual privacy?

There are many benefits to altar calls for mainstream churches—and they are all connected, in diverse ways, to the beauty of the dance of faith. In a spectrum of responses to the gospel, we find room for the many different kinds of personalities in our churches. We are not all dry and rational and "repressed," despite the victory of that image among us. "God's frozen people" is not a cliché for nothing.

Oddly, the more enthusiastic people already among us are more than ready to "shout" on behalf of their faith. What they need is cultural and social permission. While I do not believe that giving these personality types permission to shout will result in an actual shout, I do believe it would legitimate more whispering in public about what and who God really is to us. Mainstream people need to get their feet wet—not get drowned in more passionate responses to the gospel. Five possible altar calls to help them do this are:

1. Spiritual Conversion: We need to realize the different ways we understand what has happened to us when God touches our life. This is more a *spiritual* matter than a *how-*

to matter. When we understand salvation as an experience worth shouting about and worth selling, we only begin to touch its real meaning for our lives. Shouting and selling are our normal responses to joy; so why not shout and sell salvation? Specifically, when we are saved we know that we live fundamentally for and with God. We practice the presence of God.

2. Stewardship and Membership: People who have been saved empty their pocketbooks for God. An essential altar call is revising our notion of stewardship and church membership. When we legitimate stewardship and tithing expectations, we go a long way toward responding to the holy. We show people how to use the language of money for God. Salvation lets us be braver in speech with each other about money in and outside the church.

Ten percent of any church needs to be the active, asking for stewards at any time—and not just for the sake of the church budget but also for the sake of the church spirit. Leaving money out of the picture of transforming faith is a serious injury to faith. Pastors can have expanded roles in the solicitation for money. Denominations can provide training sessions, for both pastors and laypeople, that involve practicing the request. The principle is nonviolence in stewardship: we do not invade so much as offer. My experience is that people are really waiting to be asked.

Membership rules need to be both flexible and firm. One class each year is simply not enough to engage people when their hearts have been warmed. We need ongoing member classes that invite and engage different people in different ways, mentor membership, and grow disciples slowly over time. "The Holy Spirit does not wait for membership rules, . . . and a transforming moment is not necessarily taken care of by a seven week members' class, offered late next spring," according to Ben Watts, pastor of a growing and thriving Baptist church in

New London, Connecticut.[1] We can announce in many different ways that, once a heart is warmed, a person can expect the pastor or deacon to engage in immediate prayer and study with them. Members should not be required to tithe so much as expected to tithe. There is a difference, and the experience of salvation makes that difference in people's lives. Specifically, when we are saved we want to give our money away.

3. Faith Sharing: We can also encourage a private kind of response to the gospel, even if our wider goal is a less privatized faith. Intimacy is not the enemy of community; it is its foundation.

We can ask people to offer promises to share their faith, if not with another member of the church, then at least with a friend or family member in the coming week or month. This promise might include some form of accountability. For example, a card, without a name, could be placed in the offering briefly telling how the person shared his or her faith. The old-fashioned word for this type of altar call is *witnessing*.

Research shows that people return to faith within six months of a personal crisis (for example, illness, death, job loss or change, loss of a relationship). They are looking for resolution to that crisis and for help from God for that crisis. As the church, we need to offer that help immediately in a more delineated way and to encourage them in intimate speech about spirituality as well as crisis. In other words, people who are saved share their faith with each other.

4. Small Groups: Another altar call could include promises to join groups of people who share faith together by maintaining the warmth of the original touch from God. These small groups already need to be in place in the church—and ready and open to accepting new people. Adult baptism, long courses, refresher courses, and short courses, can all be done in the context of the wider church as well as the parochial church, if the parochial church thinks it has too few demands. Small groups can develop both their inward reach and their outward reach. Members within small groups can help each other witness, or they can develop literature that can be used by others outside the group who are experiencing a faith transformation. For example, if a newcomer or potential new member tells the pastor that he or she has been deeply moved by the service or that "It was like God was talking straight to me today," a trained deacon or small group member should be ready to help the person move deeper in the faith process, if the pastor is unavailable. In the absence of a real person and a real conversation, small wallet-size cards covering various topics could be distributed, and individuals could use them during the week to help think through their faith and their commitments to it. Saved people are part of a small, intimate, safe group in which they can share their faith—and their doubts—along the way.

5. Structuring a Church for a Purpose. Too many of our churches have gone committee crazy. At present, there is a great need to repurpose our board and committee structure so that salvation has a better chance of being experienced within the church. In this area, several streamlined structures will be recommended. Their focus will be on the experience of the holy. Within these alternative structures, practical matters are not eliminated so much as elevated.

Christians are the people of the incarnation, of the word become flesh, of heaven come to earth, of Christ born in Bethlehem. Christians, in general, do not despise the practical or the real; we believe, rather, that it carries God to us. Rare, however, is the committee meeting that feels that way. Here practical solutions are given to reform committees and church structures on behalf of our holy mission:

11

bringing the good news of salvation to our members. In this particular case, saved people attend meetings that are vibrant and alive with the power of God.

To implement a program of altar calls, these five calls must be developed in conjunction with a deacon (phrase used ecumenically to represent that portion of the membership authorized to do spiritual development within the congregation). Without their support or permission giving, this type of ministry will not survive. This program works the best when begun after a churchwide retreat where people show one another that they want to be more churchlike in their daily practice. The calls would come directly out of an analysis of privatized faith and are usually followed by an implementation program that shows how an average mainstream church can develop altar calls over a year's planning period. The purpose is to genuinely prepare for church growth in numbers and in faith. The first several attempts may or may not be successful, but people who are saved are less likely to fear failure than others are.

An all-church retreat offers the chance to develop the "baby steps" of salvation. No large journey can be accomplished all at once. Customizing the small steps that move a church into a collective capacity to respond to the gospel is crucial. No author can tell a church how to do these things: the steps must emerge from the church and its leadership. They must also change over time in an ongoing, dynamic process of development, evaluation, and conversation. The following structure, though, may help guide your steps.

The first retreat leads to an evaluative retreat in another year; that retreat evaluates and revises the original plan. Each organization within the church can be involved, on a regular—during its monthly meeting, for example—and prayerful basis, in a fifteen-minute review of the altered plan.

Any group gathered in the church should ask itself five simple questions, based on the five altar calls:

1. Are we practicing the presence of God today or tonight? How?
2. Are we bringing our money with us? How? Are we bringing

our time to God? How? Stewardship is not just time and not just money, but both.
3. Are we sharing our faith with others? How? For example, did our last newsletter sound like it was sent by a church that knew salvation? Did we speak to someone about what we know of God?
4. Did we participate in a small group experience, formal or informal, where more of what we know of God was revealed to us and to others? Are we being intentional about growing in our faith?
5. Did these alterations in our life result in an intentionality? Are we organizing ourselves to really be the people of God? How?

These kinds of questions can constitute staff evaluations, retreats, small groups, or regular committee meetings. We can even take them for a walk or a swim, personally, and use them as a set of guideposts for our life.

In summary form, a checklist of the first five altar calls is:

1. **The Saved Way:** the constant practice of the presence of God.

2. **Stewardship:** the giving away of significant parts of ourselves.

3. **Witnessing:** sharing the faith in simple ways.

4. **Group Practice:** intentional participation in a group that we trust enough to let them change us (mutual accountability to real individuals).

5. **Foundation Building:** intentional structuring of a church for God.

The second set of altar calls is, by necessity, more personal. These calls talk about altered people, members, disciples. They are more about what we do alone than what we do together, but they make the outer, and communal, work possible. These calls include:

1. **Keep Sabbath**
2. **Study Scripture**
3. **Pray**
4. **Act for mission**
5. **Become deeply hospitable**

Through these responses to our salvation, we become genuinely available to one another, at church, at home, and in the world.

These more private and more personal practices are not lacking in the communal at all; rather they are the foundation of the communal, just as stewardship is a public act to support a joint venture that builds from the individual's cash flow. The second five altar calls lead to altered churches but start in altered individuals. "Altered" here means a sacramental understanding of church life, the way we light a candle on an altar to announce that something is now different.

Purposing and repurposing is the foundational individual and social action of the altered life. If the reason for deepening responses to the Holy is to maintain our size and influence, we should not do it. The time has come for us to become small, to live small, to act small. Conversely, one of the key aspects of our old "imperial" Protestantism was to act big. Walter Brueggemann makes it very clear that there are at least three First Testament images for church. One is the *Davidic*, or temple-based people; the other is *wilderness*; and the third is *alternative community*. We talk a lot about wilderness, but we may actually be moving out of wilderness into an alternative community. With regard to numbers we do not act like alternative communities so much as temple-based people! We are preoccupied with the declining size of our congregations. Salvation removes that absorption on behalf of a larger concentration, that of *mission* and *ministry*.

Management consultants argue that organizations need a time line: they should innovate in their growth period, maintain in their settled period, and die when it is time to die. If our church is only trying to grow to share the load of institutional maintenance, rather than mission or ministry, we should pack our bags and leave our setting. Let someone else take over. Hearts are warmed to God all over every neighborhood in every town and city. It is not good stewardship for us to occupy spaces and places that others could use for the glory of God. Such occupation is an insult to our founders and our endowments. Moreover, serious consideration of the purpose of our endowments and property dedications is in order. Once a church decides to be for God in their ministry and not just for growth, however, then altar calls and methods of development can be implemented.

The first stage in developing an altar call program is *confession*. We have to repurpose and experience God in our repurposing. Moreover, our own souls have to warm. If they do, we can carry out any programmatic response. If they do not warm, it is time for us to turn off the lights and close up shop. The key questions, then, concern purpose: *What does God want from us, here and now? Are we focused now on the source or on true joy? Are our hearts fixed on God as our true source?*

After a few people (you do not need everybody) get excited inside the church, the basis for redemption is established, and the program has a chance of succeeding. However, we must be aware that there are serious barriers to the Holy in the human heart but that there are ways to respond to them.

Overcoming the Ten Barriers to Evangelism

1. **Fear of rejection**—and an understanding that some folk may have to go. We may need a "backdoor revival." While this consequence is risky and difficult, it is clearly more important than not preaching the word of God.
2. **People fear they are not gifted with faith.** Sometimes all they need is a spiritual partner to show them what they do have. Deacons in particular are scared that their "little" faith may be "outed" in a deaconry meeting!
3. **Simply ask the question about public commitment.** When was the last time you made a public commitment? See what happens, not judgmentally but

hopefully. It has been said by many that "the gospel is the permission and commandment to enter difficulty with hope." Don't ask people as though you know the answer. Let them answer.

4. **Acknowledge that people may have a lack of experience of the Holy.** Simply acknowledge it.
5. **Express our fears about emotionalism.**
6. **Have fun joking about how we are too sophisticated.**
7. **Acknowledge that people may be uncertain about the gospel.** Give people a card with talking points about God. When did they first learn about God? How has their faith changed from then to now? How does the gospel affect their lives? How do they teach their children about their faith?
8. **Maybe we need a slogan.** Use the talking points to get to one.
9. **Acknowledge the lack of skills.** Don't be afraid of the words, I don't know how.
10. **Make sure the pastor has authority without being authoritarian.** Don't be afraid of criticism. It is often the site of the Holy Spirit's work.
11. **Acknowledge the fear of manipulation.** Yes, there are many charlatans afoot. There is as much damage done to the gospel by silence, however, as there is done by charlatans.
12. **Acknowledge that we may need new words.** "Evangelical" may be lost—perhaps use "Holy Spirit" instead.

In general give people permission to speak about God in their lives. Help them see that their words don't have to be big or fancy.[2]

Ben Watts, professor of Evangelism, Hartford Seminary

Once we have moved the church through a transformative period, usually involving both a confessional and a critical statement of the lost sense of the Holy among us, we can change the pattern of meetings themselves. Let each deaconry meeting be a chance to testify in simple ways: have meetings be half business and half prayer, testimony, and Bible study—regularly. If the church leaders express a sense of "not knowing" the gospel well enough to confess it, there are many excellent new introductory curricula (for example, the English *Alpha*, which is quite popular, as well as a half dozen others). One little step is a lot better than any big, sure to fail steps.

After at least a year of repatterning the church leadership, congregations begin to realize that growing churches do less busy work and more building of the body work. Responsive churches do less during their transformative period. This less includes: new people are not invited to be more active but rather to rest. Burnout is avoided by making the church more lean at the level of activity while developing the underused spiritual and worshiping muscles. In some instances, churches reduce the number of programs offered or look at ways to trim the number of members on standing committees (by changing their bylaws to seat six instead of twelve people on standing committees, for example).

Altered churches never use new people to support old structure. When a church is becoming new or approaching the altered state, people—whether they are long-standing members or new ones—become renewed and need to make their own way and their own structures.

Renewed or altered churches go through a several year process to reorient themselves to the Holy. They get a new mission, and sometimes even a new mission statement. For most people, *mission statement* means a piece of white paper on which several points are enumerated and articulated. Goals, then, give birth to measurable objectives, and people get wildly bored. We also envision a long, careful, democratic process, which many find cumbersome because surely it will interfere with free time or prayer life.

We may need to begin to think of fluid or shifting missional statements, since God may be on the move as well. A mission statement may also be a nub or nodule in the heart—more like the personal mission statement of Stephen Covey, an "efficiency" guru who wrote a best-selling series on the habits of effective people, rather than something corporate and written down. It may be a bottom line at the pit of our stomach. It may be written in the sky or on a star. It may be written as a vision as opposed to an inscription in a file drawer.

We could find power for our purpose as religious institutions in the cloud land theory of patterned irrepeatability, where one very tiny difference can change an entire pattern. Meteorologists call this the "butterfly effect." In this theory, the air disturbed by the wings of a butterfly can and does change the weather around the world. Little things mean a lot.

In this scientific understanding, our small actions, our small meetings, and our small asking could find themselves deeply reconnected to each other and to the gospel. Once that connection comes, the altar calls will follow, almost automatically. Little actions on behalf of the gospel could mean big winds—or little winds, lovingly spirited.

Larger changes flow from smaller changes. Churches may have to let go of any number of assumptions beyond growth as good, such as the eleven o'clock hour for worship, the collection plate for cash (why not VISA?), the youth group on Sunday nights, or the organ as emperor of music. Churches need to think about what this generation needs by way of religious formation, and churches need to acknowledge that they simply do not have either the Sunday school formation or the foreign missions orientation that their forebears had.

What this futuristic outlook suggests is an uncanny disrespect for history; at the same time, people's chief complaint is alienation or scatteredness or lack of focus or the need for some grounding "somewhere." The church is being called to the new physics or emerging fluidity at an astonishing pace. Will the elders need to be sacrificed for this fluidity to appear? I think not. If the fluidity means anything at all, or has any moral capacity, it will be able to include the past in its flow. Right now, so many of the battles in churches are intergenerational. They represent the strength of the past and the future in a tug-of-war. Conceivably a nonviolent or mending approach to the demands of the emerging future will allow us to give our attention to the future without demeaning our current pew sitting constituency any more than they already feel demeaned. Foundational experiences of the Holy, like those experienced by many of our people long ago in church, are not to be sneered at. Rather, they are to be repeated.

If Letty Russell is right that ministry is nonhierarchical partnership—hear the mending and connecting—then all constituencies have a place at the table. Mission statements need to include the words *mend, tie,* or *connect.* They need to avoid the diabolical dualisms of "bold, new future" versus "old, stupid past." Ask the Native Americans; they can explain this conundrum to us. The elders are part, not *not* part, of the future!

When we talk about revering the past, however, we have to make sure that it is the spiritual past, not the cultural past. Culture has a funny way of trying to make itself eternal when it is the most relative of all matters. Unfortunately, many mainstream churches are so enmeshed in the culture wars between the so-called right and left wings that God cannot get in the door.

Getting over lost imperialism means getting over lost categories and lost dualism. Two different categories can help frame the paradigm shift. *One set is open or closed.* I have known open right-wing people and closed left-wing people and vice versa. Whether we can open our conceptual frameworks to each other, to the past, or to the future, these are the questions that matter—not political name-calling. *Another set is fluid or fixed.* You will hear the new physics coming in. Fluid is fixed, if we buy what the new physicists are telling us. Fluid is ontologic. Open is ontologic. It is quite possible that we could shift the color of the battle—and burst the violent paradigm of right and left—by substituting these words in the bases of our mission.

Growth may or may not result from fluidity or openness, but the gospel will be protected. It will enjoy its right size. Our hearts will be warmed by it. The response to the word is both liturgically and practically absent in mainline churches. We do take up an offering, and we do offer a doxology. But these are perfunctory more than passionate. Rare is the invitation to *spiritual transformation* or *extended commitment* or a *long-term process of becoming altered.*

Now we institutionally prefer the privatized faith so much that an external response is considered embarrassing: no one should know how we are responding to the word of God. That is "between us and our God," despite the fact that worship is corporate and churches are communities and beggars everywhere are begging for bread.

A few simple altar calls, instituted after a congregations' leaders genuinely hear the word of God, can go a long way toward deprivatizing faith and spreading the gospel. There is no time line to the altar. But the altar and the Holy can and will guide us every step of the way, especially if we are willing to be slowly, carefully, and surely led.

Chapter 1

Salvation as a Response to the Holy

◆ ◆

When God comes into our life, we are saved. We are saved from one-dimensional thinking, we are safe from fear, we are securely removed from the petty and the small, and we are at peace. *Shalom* is the Hebrew word for this combination of personal and global security, this peace that passes human understanding, this removal from what so many people erroneously think is real.

Salvation is from the same root word as safety, security, and *shalom*. It is a big word, almost too big for humans. But once we have the experience of the holy in our lives, it seems to be almost too small. We *know* things after we are touched by the presence of God that we did not know beforehand. We are not confused when we are told to "get real" or come back to the "real" world; we know the reality of God's world and how richly it supersedes the one we used to think was real.

A confirmand once refused confirmation after taking all the course work and fulfilling all the requirements. She explained to the pastor that "when God comes into our lives, for real, everything is changed. . . . I'm just not ready for that." She preferred the ordinary placement of God, in a corner called Sunday, in a place accessible only by a spiritual remote. We push a button, and God comes in; we push another button, and we are back on one of the more popular stations.

Some churches hold altar calls, which are very public rituals after a service of worship in which a person who is called by the "altar" comes forward and agrees to be saved. In this book, we are going to unpack the meaning of salvation, that "altared" state in which we are different. We are going to take salvation off our spiritual shelf and out

21

of our spiritual suitcase, piece by piece, and talk about some of the things that happen to people who are saved. We are going to issue an altar call and show some ways that real people can respond to the reality of the call from the Holy One.

An African American colleague often speaks of the "required" obedience of coming to the altar at the end of the service. He worries that sometimes it is a phony obedience. Perhaps it is, but how can someone tell whether the Holy One has visited another person? Here we will speak of ways we respond when we are touched by the Holy—not set up new requirements for response.

Salvation is not a formularized experience. Beware of people who carry formulas around! Most saved people do not even understand the peace they experience. Saved people are not haunted and hounded by the trivial: they know a larger, deeper, and more significant dimension. The daily experience or what Ada Maria Isasi-Diaz understands appropriately as the site of salvation, *lo quotidiano*,[1] is real, but it does not fill all the space in our lives. Saved people experience fear but they also experience freedom from their fear—both, not just the one: not just the triumph of fear but the triumph of peace over fear. There is still a daily, but it is a deeper daily. The formerly trivial sits inside the holy and befriends it.

"Do you accept Jesus Christ as your Lord and Savior?" is the way the question is usually asked in those churches that issue a call from the altar after a service. The candidate responds, "Yes, I do." Here, we broaden this fundamentally important question to ask it in a larger framework: Do you accept that what you have experienced is God touching your life? God, ever so broadly, means the Holy, the Sacred, the Transcendent, the Good. This broad definition does not exclude the power of the traditional call so much as it adds to it. We are talking about Christianity plus not Christianity alone.

When you experience the sacred, you may experience Jesus as Christ in that experience—or just Jesus, or just God, or just something utterly nameless. Both Christians and non-Christians know God in named and unnamed ways. Our interest here is much more in what we do after we are touched by the sacred than in accurately naming the sacred. We are interested in the response to the holy, not the nature of the Holy. I switch the capital case on purpose. Some experiences of God are grand and rich and large; others are small and almost too little to mention out loud, much less parade to the altar and commit to in public. The goal, then, is to allow small as well as large experiences of God to be spiritually legitimate. Yes, there are spiritual police out there in full uniform: they fill up our brains with definitions of what counts as salvation. We have to be very careful not to let them do so.

For a long time, many Americans have hoped for the big knock at the door. God may be making big sounds all the time, and we may not have the permission to hear them.

Altar call is too narrow a focus for commitment responses and disciplines. Nevertheless, it is the call to the altar, to the holy—to the holy in a simple, doable way—that I want to focus on. I want to punctuate the experience of transformation that salvation brings: the "altared" state. I want to show how we keep the Holy in our lives after we have experienced it. While I have nothing against the mystical experience and nothing but praise for the original experience, because it is often so profound and life changing, I know the Holy does not remain without a little patterning of our response to it. God may touch our lives once or twice in actual experience, but if we do not worship, pray, read, associate, give—in other words, respond to that call—we are likely to be only halfway home. William James described those of us who understand the necessity of patterned response as those who are not just born again but born again and again. We are the "twice born." Maybe even the thrice and more born.

Eugene Peterson speaks of the habit of reading the Bible as being life changing over time. This lifelong response to the Holy is my focus here; I do not mind the single mountaintop experience, but I like the daily even more.

Just as I move back and forth between big and little experiences of the sacred, I also move back and forth between "we" and "they." We, even I, know salvation. They, many more in number, know salvation as well—if not more profoundly. What knowledge I have about responses to the Holy is mine—plus. It is not just mine. I have observed more of it in others than in myself. I have known a few mountaintops, and they have caused me to lose my breath. I have also known *lo quotidiano,* the beauty of walking daily with God, of singing, "Only Thou Art Holy" on a subway car, or praying, "Nearer my God to thee, nearer to thee" while washing dishes.

The patterned responses to the experience of salvation will include, but not be limited to, the daily. We will speak of tithing or how we use our money to respond to the God of and in our lives. Tithing will join the keeping of the Sabbath, or how we use our time in general, as simple, if obvious, methods of responding to the holy, of saying yes to the call we have heard at whatever altar we have heard it. We will also consider evangelism, what we in my denomination, the United Church of Christ (UCC), have come to call the "e word" for people who do not think they are evangelical. How do we politely introduce others to our faith experiences? How do we tell what we know of the holy without using a hammer, but with the love that we knew in the Holy when it first touched us?

The focus is the *response* to the holy. Right now those of us in mainline churches are a little like an interrupted African chant: there is a call but no response in our music. Some of the problem is in the call—pastors do not really know how to speak it as well as we might—but most of the problem is in the response and getting it to the right size.

Commitment of any kind scares people, but it need not. Commitment is what saves us from fear of God. When we commit to the experience that we have of God, we are saved. Commitment is often a heavy word in our society, said by the "should" crowd to the leisure crowd. A part of what we want to do in responding to the holy is reclaim the word *commitment.*

Once we know we are saved, safe, secure, at peace, how do we behave? What do we look like after we are saved? What picture of self was the confirmand mentioned earlier attempting to avoid? What new commitments do we have? These are the questions that interest us here.

The problem is a question of proportion or size. The call from the Holy is a call to commitment. We live in a commitment averse society, in a commitment averse age. Say the word *commitment,* and people groan. They feel overcommitted already. They speak of their budget as already spent; they feel they have no discretionary income. They speak of living in a time famine, with all time already committed. There is not a sense of space for God. Thus God gets the corner, the extra, the remote.

But salvation is an entirely different experience. It is part of our insurance bill, part of our daily work, part of the laundry we fold late at night. God is not so much extra as *incarnate*, that is God is within the person we already are. God's commitment to us is so profound and thoroughgoing that once we are aware of it, we cannot help responding in a committed way.

Achieving a sense of proportion and right size about the word *commitment* takes us a long way toward understanding what it means to be saved. The call from the altar is a call from God. It is a form of commitment, in that it is God's commitment to us. Commitment comes from connection, and connection feels overwhelming, too large—often even grandiose. To reestablish commitment and response to the Holy in our lives, we have to right-size both our connections and our commitments.

We start in amazement: God is too connected to us not to be committed to us. Even after we neglected the glory of the Creation, left Eden, trashed the tablets and the tablet giver, endured a flood and found a rainbow in the sky—even after God sent Jesus, his only child, those of you who have or work with children know what a commitment that is—even after all this and more, God stays connected to humanity. God cannot sever the connection with humanity; that is what we mean by commitment: a refusal to sever connection.

Evelyn Underhill speaks of God's love of humanity as a joy that cannot be altered by any trial. She speaks of her own faith as that same joy. Nothing can separate her from the love of God, which is in Christ Jesus. This commitment of God to us and God to joy and us to God and us to joy is what constitutes the nature of the response to the Holy. There is limitless love. There are no contingencies, no bargains, no barriers over which God's love cannot jump.

Many find this absence of contingencies very hard to understand. There has been a sea change in the way commitment is understood in our society. Consider nursing; it has long been considered a committed and connected profession. Daniel Chambliss's *Beyond*

Caring: Hospitals, Nurses, and the Social Organization of Ethics is a study of nursing ethics. Chambliss contends that ethics is often too narrowly described; by focusing on what is right and wrong, ethics ignores important questions about the social structures in which we act. In the case of nursing, for example, a number of features of the structure serve to blunt or change normal ethical reactions: crisis becomes routine in the emergency room, and structures that blunt nurses' reactions are set up so that nurses can keep caring for patients' bodies, which are thereby rendered profane rather than sacred.

While Western ethics often assumes that the core issue is uncertainty about what to do, Chambliss contends that the basic problem for nurses is not such intrapsychic dilemmas or uncertainty. Rather, they know what is right or wrong, but they do not always have the authority to follow through on what they know. Moreover, their professional training leads them to identify their primary role as one of caring, but within the hospital structure, nurses are generally subordinate to others and must often obey orders (this, of course, differs depending on the nurse's position in the hospital). The real dilemma, then, is not personal uncertainty concerning what to do but something more like the following lament: I want to do good, but my boss won't let me. Likewise in *lo quotidiano*, we experience an absence of the power of God in us.

Saved people have the capacity for ethics. Saved people find the power they need in their salvation. Salvation is the missing ingredient that makes the good possible in us and through us. Salvation is the borrowing of God's power for our days: altar calls are the promissory note we sign saying, "Yes, we will do what is right." What is right is staying open and in relationship to God; ethics flows from that relationship. Right and wrong, on their own, are impossible.

Commitment is experienced as blocked by the structures in which we worship. We want to humanize each other, but we are forgetting how to do it. We want to connect with each other, but we do not know how. The problem with commitment is that we do not know how to connect. We want to do what is right, but we do not know how. The nurse's dilemma is a metaphor for church members' lack of response to the call of the Holy. Frequently, church members go to church to connect to the Holy, but they often leave with these words: I don't know how.

Some call this ethical dilemma "moral distress." Moral distress arises when one knows the right thing to do, but institutional constraints make it nearly impossible to pursue the right course of action.

When it comes to commitment and the members of our churches, people know what they should do, but they do not do it. They do not feel they have the power to do it. They should know their Bible. They do not. They should pray. They do not. They should attend worship regularly. Many do not. There is a culture of shame about church membership that is similar to the culture of shame in many work sites, like nursing.

The invocation of these "shoulds" only makes the matter worse. The shoulds of traditional authority no longer hold sway. In what Lawrence Friedman, a Yale law professor, calls "the horizontal society,"[3] we form groups of like-minded individuals who find their identity through the ironic but persistent authorities of mass culture. In the horizontal society—a virtual reality where traditional social hierarchies no longer rule—our sense of identity has been irretrievably altered. In his book of the same name, Friedman argues that ties of vertical authority—the ties that attach us to parents, bosses, heads of state, priests, and others—have weakened. As a result, society is more horizontal than in the past. Salvation is about vertical relationships, but it is very hard to have vertical relationships in an increasingly horizontal society.

But the experience of the Holy is not just vertical; it is vertical and more than vertical. Because the Holy is so often perceived (falsely) as vertical only, the Holy is not connecting to us nor we to it. Again, salvation is what makes us capable of connecting to each other. We have the love we need to risk connection. Our connection to God lets us connect to others. We know that real life is not just on this horizontal level; real life is also a matter of something that touched us from above, and affected our deepest below, that thing we call our gut.

Religious institutions live in an intentional institutional lag: we hold on to the vertical in the horizontal. This does not mean we are

27

estranged from the horizontal as a vehicle for the holy as many fear. Were we able to issue altar calls consistent with our incarnational faith—which says that God is both transcendent and immanent, both near and far, both horizontal and vertical—we could right-size our responses.

Religious institutions are the ideal people to manage what the pundits call "glocalization," the ability to live well and connected in the global village. Salvation makes glocalization possible. Here people have the power to commit to God and each other, to commit face-to-face and far away.

The horizontal identity creates a feeling that anything is possible—when actually very few of us, like nurses, have much real power at all. As Friedman explains, let loose from our traditional vertical moorings and exposed—through television and the Internet—to an array of fascinating celebrities and ways of life, we feel we can transcend the boundaries of our primary identity, such as gender, religion and race, and carve out new identities. The horizontal identity is wholly dependent on people deciding to associate. Prompted by what is on our screens, we reach out and, for example, see the latest Spielberg film or join a Save the Seals organization. At the same time we are less attached to more traditional institutions, such as our community or church.

The real problem with the horizontal identity, which Friedman only implies, is that in terms of true stability, we are stranded in a widening gyre, in William Butler Yeats's words, where the falcon cannot hear the falconer. Response and call separate.

Finally, arguably, our bond with ourselves is disintegrating. Similarly, our bond with God breaks. When connection is lost, commitment becomes impossible. Salvation, in restoring connection to God, restores our capacity for commitment.

Most people live in great frustration with their lack of connection with each other—and subliminally, with their God. Can you remember the last time you had technology rage? We live with "You have mail," "Push one, one for a real person," and delete buttons. What happens when the screen gets internalized? Life, God, relationship, commitment, and connection get too small—all the while they are being made to seem more grandiose.

Interior life shrinks. Because of the illusion of enormous power and the reality of very little power and because of increasingly unsupported institutionally interior lives, anger and confusion become the place where most people live. This helps explain the anxiety that pervades society. It has reached our children: three million elementary school children are now on Ritalin or other anxiety-disorder drugs. In 1990 it was three thousand. This "narrowing of our interiority" contributes to the disconnectedness of Friedman's horizontal society. "Social Capitals"—neighborhoods, networks, relatives, churches, temples—are much smaller than they once were. They cause people to become more pessimistic about human nature.[4]

Whatever the causes—television, technology, economics—the results are a disaster, says Wendy Donner, associate professor of philosophy at Carleton University. She says that while getting rid of constraining vertical structures has brought us many pluses—such as a more critical, open society—we are under a great illusion if we think this is all we need to be free. We need certain vertical structures whether they are public education or stronger family ties or what I call salvation. People cannot be committed to something that they cannot be connected to.

Through altar calls, we can begin to right-size the response to the gospel. We can take account of the ways that commitment has changed, in the horizontal society and moral distress, caused by the two-career family and the lack of time (perceived and real) that people face. Over time we can rebuild the lost intermediate structures through simple, doable steps.

We need to recognize that people are actually responding to the Holy in their lives. However, their responses need affirmation, since they may not fit into traditional pictures of piety or church membership. People meditate. They exercise. They read self-help books. These are actually devotional practices—but many still see them as only secular. Chaos theorists understand these disconnections; butterflies are fluttering all over the place and causing various *unseen* effects. Like the effects of the butterflies, people's responses to the Holy are not seen. These responses, which we are not hearing, not seeing, not responding to, are happening but we do not recognize or acknowledge them.

The route out of moral distress may be to see the ways people are connecting in the covenant (that big word for the unseverable connection between God and humanity) to each other and to understand that neither we nor they see or hear these responses. Blindness and deafness are common enough themes in Jesus' teaching. He also heals the deaf and the blind. Let those who have eyes see, he says.

We must begin to talk about responses to the holy as *call* and *commitment* and *connection*—and try to develop a sense of proportion that makes sense to the people in this middle passage in disconnected time and space.

Sample Altar Call: The Saved Way

One question can guide our lives together and our life alone: Are we practicing the presence of God, or What would God want me to do here? This question needs to penetrate both our conscious and our unconscious lives. It is a way of living our eternity now.

When the conversation in a meeting turns sour and hopeless, are we able to see the despair with God's eyes? If we find ourselves in a rote repetition of the Lord's Prayer or singing without our heart and soul present, is there a way we can remember to whom we are speaking? If we get hurt or someone we love gets hurt, can we find the comfort of our Companion?

Functional atheism prevails. Too much of our life *pretends* that God is present rather than acts as though God is present. When we practice the presence of God, we do not act as if God is present. We act *with* God's presence.

Chapter 2

Money as a Call from and to the Altar

◆ ◆

A man dies and goes to heaven. Of course, Saint Peter meets him at the Pearly Gates. Saint Peter says, "Here's how it works: You need one hundred points to make it into heaven. You tell me all the good things you've done, and I give you a certain number of points for each item—depending on how good it was. When you reach one hundred points, you get in."

"Okay," the man says. "I was married to the same woman for fifty years and never cheated on her, even in my heart."

"That's wonderful," says Saint Peter. "That's worth three points!"

"Three points?" he says. "Well, I attended church all my life and supported its ministry with my tithe and service."

"Terrific!" says Saint Peter. "That's certainly worth a point."

"One point? I started a soup kitchen in my city and worked in a shelter for homeless veterans."

"Fantastic, that's good for two more points," he says.

"Two points!" the man cries. "At this rate the only way I will get into heaven is by the grace of God."

"Bingo! One hundred points!" cried Saint Peter, "Come on in!"

When we are saved, we do not think of God as a point keeper or of tithing as a point; we do not accumulate points to get to heaven. We are already there. We already live in a kind of heaven, a kind of deep security into which, and from which, no harm can come. When we are saved, we want to give away what we have. We no longer need it as much. We still pay our bills and buy sale items at the grocery store. We do not squander our money. Instead, we steward it.

By steward I mean to treasure deeply—using money for God in

31

the same way we use ourselves for God. We do not have a place where God is not—so we do not keep a "nest egg" or need to start one.

Often, we find a tithe too limiting: Only 10 percent? When salvation assures us, we no longer value money so highly. It becomes a part of the package of our life and reduces its percentage of importance. When we are saved, money moves out of the point system and into the praise system.

The moral distress we so often feel is due to the fact that we would like to do the right thing but do not know how and we would like to live without anxiety about money but do not know how. That anxiety dissolves when God becomes most important in our lives. It becomes a small anxiety compared to the large assurance that we know.

Point systems are not to be laughed at. They are good ways through moral distress. They give us something measurable and accomplishable to do. That is why a tithe is so comforting: it gives us an historical foundation for our giving. It answers the question of how much and does so without judgment. For most middle-class Americans, it is easy to stay well fed, even after we give away 10 percent. We do not need to feel guilty about how much we have, even after we tithe—instead, we may dare to be grateful for our abundance and the capacity to give abundantly.

For those of us who cannot afford to give away 10 percent, there is no need to worry about God feeling cheated. There is easily 10 percent of *ourselves*, even if it is not in a checkbook, that we can give away. There is probably even more than 10 percent.

So often our temptation, when we face our moral distress, is to reduce things to something manageable and doable. Tithing can be good or bad—depending on how we do it. If it is part of the point system, better we hang on to our money and live by God's grace. But if our tithe is a genuine response to the grace we already know, whatever we give will be fine. The reason? We will give enough once we are saved.

There is almost no such thing as an American who can accept the reality of our privilege. It is too large. When we speak of using money as a way to express our experience of the Holy, we find several tempting reductions. "I'll just tithe, and everything will be fine." Yes, things will be fine. But tithing alone will not handle money for those of us who are truly saved. When we are saved, we will not care about money's exchange value so much. We will care about what God wants to do with it. Like Schindler in *Schindler's List*, we will wish we had sold the car to save a few more people: we will not have the need to hold on to what we have.

We will not only be tempted by reductive strategies, we will also be tempted by premature resolution so that we never have to think about money in connection with God again. Some of us will try to resolve the matter once and for all. An absolute amount will be decided; a rigorous plan will be instituted. Then our income will change—up or down: someone in our own family will need our money or we will get a big raise or a big bonus. Now last year's percentage is this year's problem.

Saved people often tithe, which means giving away 10 percent of our income. Saved people often want to give more than that, but they cannot because of their own family or job situation. The Jewish law of tzedakah shows a good way to think about tithing and the necessity for it to be fluid and responsive to our own personal situation. In ascending order of value, we take care of ourselves first, our relatives second—so that we need not be dependent ourselves—and for the poor and the public third. The highest good in this law is to give something away to another who needs it—and have the other not even know who the donor is. This hierarchy is no doubt the Hebrew source of Jesus' adulation of the widow and her quiet mite. Tithes, in this sense, are part of the highest good. We give to those we do not even know because we want to give to them. We want to give to them because we cannot forget how much God, whom we love, loves them.

When we are saved, we can risk change and fluidity in our pattern of giving. We can risk being changed by our relationship with God. We can risk alteration. We can give away more or less and not be full of fear about doing the wrong thing. Instead of resolution or reduction, we will enjoy acceptance, whatever we do will be fine with our God, and relinquishment, the marvelous capacity to give up worrying.

When French postmodern philosophers speak of the insurrection of subjugated knowledges, by which they mean the raising of voices by those who are not ordinarily heard, I often sneak in a thought about God. Everything in the world is constantly trying to tell us to worry about money: we are revolutionary when we do not. It is God's action in us that lets us not worry about money, at least not about our own.

There is so much guilt surrounding the matter of money that we have to strip away centuries of layers of paintlike substances just to get to the place where we can be clear, much less "refinished." Money tells us who we are too much of the time! But when we experience God telling us who we are, as God's beloved child, money gets dethroned. We become revolutionaries in a rebellion against money. We self-differentiate from the world's image of fear and anxiety about money. We paint our picture differently. We light it well so others can see it, but we do not judge others with our use of money. Our salvation is not intended to shame, but to liberate.

Is personal mastery of this proportion a possibility in this world? Absolutely. With God, nothing is impossible. We do not self-differentiate on our own. We do not master our own money on our own. God changes us so that we can.

Behaving differently about money can cause many people to be nervous. We will need careful inner work not to become self-righteous once money no longer governs our life. Again, there will be temptations. This time the temptation will be to retreat into even more privacy about money than before. Mainstream Christians are quite comfortable in a cocoon, a private enclosed place. There is no need to hide what we know about money's proper place in our life or to brag about it. Its truth will show in its own way; we simply light our paintings properly. If we are lucky, we give away what we can without letting others know we are doing it.

When our money is our own, rather than the wholly owned subsidiary of our anxiety, we are free to renew our hope for the poor. We see how God intends to save the world by helping the rich let go of their wealth. Some clergy believe that the temptation we must resist is the one that says that nothing can be done. When we are saved, we are free of that temptation.

As the old Yiddish proverb puts it, The heaviest burden is having nothing to carry. "Carry" comes from the root "to care." Saved people love God's method of saving the world: we are to carry each other. Saved people do not even mind paying taxes because taxes privilege us with mutual care. Taxes join tithes in being a part of God's plan for the full redistribution of power in the world. Many of us find it easy to be patriotic, even nationalistic, about our privilege as Americans. Saved people find their way through the muddle of both taxes and tithing.

Oddly, those who profess the maximum patriotism are often most allergic to taxes. Aversion to taxes is what is un-American; paying taxes is all-American—if by American we mean that godly dream of a nation with "liberty and justice for all." *E pluribus unum* is another version of the same hope. Grand things, like liberty and justice, are not cheap; they are expensive. Airlines and department stores can go the discounted route; liberty and justice cannot.

In my house, and maybe in yours, there is a lot of month left at the end of the money. What my husband and I earn pays mortgages, makes payments on one old van and one old car, purchases enough insurance to make anyone feel safe, and buys enough food to keep three children, and us, very well fed. Are we rich? No. We have plenty of burdens to carry, but we are not unemployed. And our money is not unemployed either.

In addition to our bills, my family has made a commitment to tithe. Through these taxes and tithes, we get to be part of the national experiment in democracy. Without these payments, we would be freeloading on the grand experiment we call America. With our tithing, we shoulder up to a delightful burden.

A checkbook is the best way to see what matters to a person or an institution. What matters to most people is national and local community. We believe these are the things that matter most to God as well. Ironically, these commitments to community enhance our personal security more than any strictly personal choice we might make. Generosity is better for our hearts than greed. Saved people understand this irony about the source of our security.

Security is less about what we have as individuals and more about what we have as a community. Even if we do not play the daily lottery—which many people falsely imagine will keep them safe if they win it—many Americans have been seduced into thinking of security as personal. We act out of its values. We imagine we would be better if we personally had more security—but we tell long stories about how far and how beautifully our grandmother spread her soup in the Depression. We need to realize that we will be better off the more we spread the soup, not the more meat we have in our bowl. We will be better off if we have more socially and less materially. Crime will reduce. Schools will be better. When we stop hoping that we too can become rich, on whatever lottery we have built our lives, we become free to be rich in and with one another. In *Love in the Time of Cholera* by Gabriel Garcia Marquez, someone accused him of being rich, and he said he was not rich, rather he was "a poor man with money. There is a difference." The opposite is also true: we can be rich people without money.

America is still a place where people "find a way when there is no way," like many grandmothers did during the Depression. It is still a place where people take what little rice and beans they have and make it into something good to give to the woman down the hall who lost her son to a gang fight. Still some poor, sick people "pay" the church first, even before the pharmacist, and find a pride in that choice that helps them get through when they have to stretch their pills. These Americans care for one another. They are rich because of it. They are responding to their salvation, whether it be Christian based or not. They know they are, somehow, in some place beyond doctrine and denomination, children of God.

Today, for whatever reason, few middle-class families question the financial need for both parents in a household to work, but a quarrel is developing between our economic security and our spiritual security. Most realize that our children are not being raised as well as they should be; we have handed our children over to a combination of baby-sitters: television, Nintendo, and video games. And we see the results of these less loving parents in the children's attitudes and behaviors. (Not that all baby-sitters are less loving than all parents, rather that parenting for money rather than love probably has consequences.) Children have less respect for parental authority precisely because they experience less parenting.

The effect of the two-career family on women is hardly more desirable. Most women report their number one problem is fatigue. The second shift after work is simply too much for the average human being. Men do not seem to be happy with their limited leisure time either. They are now taking over many aspects of the second shift, and they are less inclined to ignore household responsibilities after work than they have been in the past.

The figures are all in. Money dominates our lives. United States manufacturing employees work the equivalent of at least two months (320 hours) more than their counterparts in West Germany or France, according to Juliet Schor, a Harvard University professor and author of *The Overspent American*.[1] Furthermore, between 1969 and 1987, time on the job for the average employed American increased by 163 hours a year, or one month. Americans have paid a real price for prosperity. They have accepted longer work hours to pay for improved lifestyles, particularly since the actual earnings of hourly wage workers declined in the 1980s. Schor says that half of the U.S. population reports that they do not have enough time for their families.

This data is disturbing. We see how it hurts children, women, and men, and it puts enormous pressure on marriage itself. We also know how much it has harmed our congregations. Churches simply do not have the volunteer workforce that they used to have. With both adults in a family working for pay, it is almost cruel to invite them to a third volunteer shift, after finishing the first two shifts of work and family. Yet these evening meetings, study groups, and coffee klatches are the spice of the human spirit, the time when we go beyond worship to locate the true meaning of the gospel for our lives. It does not take long to see how much salvation—and its deeper securities are pragmatic as well as spiritual—matters.

Church attendance is also affected by these longer work hours. In my congregation, people come to worship about every other Sunday. I have asked them why, and their answer is reasonable: Because I just need some time to cool down, space out, do nothing and be nothing. It seems to me to be a good answer.

Likewise, custodial care of the sick or aging is affected by the two-career family. I know this is true for me. Casseroles that I would have delivered to a sick family in my neighborhood years ago, I don't even bake today.

When Americans explain why both adults in the family work outside the home, they say, "We have to"; we can't pay the mortgage or the car payment without two incomes. There is a reason beyond necessity. Americans, while working harder, also spend three to four times as much money a year in nonfood shopping as their counterparts in Western European countries. Schor also reports an astonishing rise in the "things" that Americans own.

I can certainly see the increase in the things in my own home. A grandfather spoke to me the other day about the history of the Christmas stocking in his Irish immigrant family. "I got an orange in my stocking. My son got an orange and a small toy in his stocking and one big toy. His son gets an orange and several small toys in his stocking—and the whole toy store." That pattern is not unusual. The economy is a silent partner at the tables in our homes yelling, feed me, feed me—like the Joads' car in *Grapes of Wrath*—and very few of us know how to get beyond this situation. Many want a simpler lifestyle, a culture of permanence and sustainability, and to work outside the home less. Few know how to get there. Again, we hear the familiar rhythms of the moral distress.

God directs us to the very power that we need to solve these matters. God gives us that power by reducing the importance of money in our lives. We become different people—people with the capacity to challenge the economy that is saddling us. Specifically, we become people who know our security is not from our money.

Three things happen in us—*psychologically, economically,* and *spiritually*—simultaneously. Each part has a dimension that is inner and outer and a dimension that connects inner to outer. For example, people with low incomes have the same promise as those with higher incomes: that their lives will not be so driven by the biological that they can have time to love themselves, regardless, according to Alice Walker. It is the same promise, a promise of freedom in shelter so that we can be free from shelter's demands. It is not that housing is not important, just that it is not all we are supposed to do or be.

Psychological freedom from money is the consequence of *spiritual freedom* from money. Once we are free, ironically, we want to make sure that everyone has enough and that no one has the control of too much. According to Gandhi, we no longer want what others cannot have. Once we are free, we become warriors for economic justice. Psychologically, spiritually, and politically we side with God's hopes for humanity, because they are also our hopes.

If you look at the great organizers of the poor, they are the same people who believe in the way things should be rather than the way things are. Such people are economically *free or mature* not economically *innocent*. Economic innocence supports itself by claiming, "This is the best of all possible worlds; nothing can be done; the rich get richer and the poor get poorer." Economic innocence covers itself in a thin layer of cynicism, which believes in the way things are rather than the way God wants things to be. God says mansion, many rooms, lively stones; the world says two bath, two bedroom, no pets, $750 a month, and no section 8. There is a difference in where we should focus our attention—spiritually, economically, and psychologically. When we are saved, we find our attention focused by God, not by money. When we are saved, we give away as much money as we can. And we enjoy doing so. We *altar* the way we understand money. We are saved from the point system, saved by grace.

Sample Altar Call: Stewardship

To respond to the gospel with stewardship means the ability to joyfully give away significant parts of ourselves—both our money and our time. To find out what really matters, look at your checkbook and your datebook. Where does God and God's world fit in?

If we cannot give away money, can we give away time? If we cannot give away time, can we give away money? How do we become intentional about the percentage of our life that we give to others? How do we determine the percentage for an activity—and stick to that percentage? Some people volunteer once a month at a shelter; often these are people without much discretionary income.

Instead they tithe their time. Other people live extraordinarily ecological lives: they do not waste. They do not forget to recycle paper or cans. They shop at thrift stores; they make sure they have little "excess" in their own homes. Stewardship is the habit of knowing that all things belong to God.

Chapter 3

Sharing Faith in a World of Holy Discontents

◆ ◆

When people experience the holy, they tell someone. They speak of their faith out loud. We *witness*. We show. We are examples. Along with witness, another old-fashioned word is *evangelism*. We witness for the Evangel, the one whom we have seen. Through us, people see God.

There are at least two kinds of evangelism; one has bad manners, the other does not. When the Southern Baptists held their annual convention in Salt Lake City, they proceeded to "evangelize" the resident members of The Church of Jesus Christ of Latter-day Saints, who tolerated their efforts with a quiet, but hostile, graciousness. It is a regular practice for the Southern Baptists, as a national body, to evangelize in every city they visit.

My feeling, however, is that the evangelization of any city is rude, and in this case the accompanying zeal, which could have been viewed as overbearing, was particularly inappropriate. There is a better way to evangelize. Self-definition works as a religious etiquette. Who is one Christian to tell another Christian that he or she is not a Christian? The Jesus Christ I worship would not step on another's toes in this way; instead, I believe he would have asked his disciples the very important question, "Who do *you* say that I am?" Speak for yourself, says my Lord. Do not speak for others. It is as bad as reaching across the table for the butter when a polite request (could you please pass . . .) would be a better option.

Not all evangelism, however, has bad manners. Some is the genuine sharing from the heart of what we know as the evangel or the Messiah or the big truth of our own small portion of large faith. We can speak about Christ softly or loudly. Spoken loudly, the very word *Christ* becomes the oppression that the genuine Christ liberates us from. We are not here to control one another, or the world; we are here to love one another. And love is different from control. If I offer what I know of God as a gift to you, I have the good manners of evangelism; if I offer what I know of God as a club against you, I have the bad manners of evangelism. The difference is control. The gospel is an urging by God that refuses control. The gospel is an appeal of love and gift.

The Southern Baptists, to an extent, were telling the Mormons that the Southern Baptists were superior. They tried to control and "improve" the Mormons. This type of behavior is not evangelism; it is control. Religious control is no prettier than political or social control. Control is control. It is also bad manners, and not Christlike.

A friend tells the story of the Reformation theologians Calvin and Zwingli. They are on their way to a major confrontation about the directions of their separate movements; they are to visit with each other the very next day. Zwingli dreams that two goats are traveling two mountain paths—ambling, walking in a deep calm. Suddenly it becomes apparent that their paths are not only going to cross but that they are going to cross at a stretch in the mountain where the pass is narrow and only one will be able to go at a time. The goats continue on their way and, sure enough, they meet. One goat lies down and allows the other to walk through the pass. Then the other goat gets up and continues on its journey. Zwingli wondered the rest of his life why his God's eye view of the goat's passage never told him which goat was his. He feared that the passing goat might have stepped on the lying goat, but it did not. It passed by. (I wonder if it said Excuse me as it passed.)

It is a great mystery why religious groups think of truth as a contest, why one has to win while the other loses. There is plenty of room on any mountain, or in any city, for both groups to be somewhat right. They do not need to knock each other off the mountain. When we make a witness to the holy, we are not making a witness to truth so much as to love. Many of us refuse the chance to witness because we know deep within ourselves that we are somewhat unsure of what we are saying, but we never need to doubt the love we know.

Moreover, religious groups need to share the gift of what they know about God with one another. That's all. They do not need to win a contest; they simply need to share what they know. That sharing is not small: it is large, and it is enough. No one gets hurt if, when we pass by each other, we use good manners. Good manners start and stop in love. Genuine witness is complex love. They'll know we are Christians by our love—or so says the familiar song. Genuine witness means showing how willing we are to move out of the safe country of right and wrong into the unsafe territory of love.

The experience of the Holy is so strong that it gives us what we need to be able to love. The experience of the Holy is so strong that it overcomes shyness and fear of rejection. Before we know God, we probably do not really know love. Once we do know God, we are truly able to love. We are even able to love the one Jesus calls our neighbor.

Today's neighbor is likely to be a very complex person, and perhaps even wholly or holy discontented or disconnected. He or she may be Moslem or Catholic, adamantly secular or bedecked in religious tattoos, angel pins, and crystals. Today's neighbors may consider themselves to be "seekers," people who are desperate for the word only they can speak. If we believe we must witness to these holy discontents from within Christianity, we will have a very hard time having good manners. If, however, we can offer a word of love, witnessing will be quite simple.

Moreover, today's neighbor is as likely to be a member of an interfaith family, "postdenominational"—beyond any single faith or origin, untutored in any faith, or part of a blended family—or a cradle-something, but no longer happy at home. Today's neighbor is just as likely to be scared of institutional religion. People increasingly speak of denominations as old and their spirituality as new. The institutional vessel seems unworthy of the voyage the faithful want to take. When we witness in this old, stade context and have no place of worship to suggest to our neighbor, we have an incredibly deinstitutionalized and disembodied task. Again, love is our salvation. We do not have to have someone come to our church to have made an effective witness. Instead, we may want to attend his or her mosque as an act of solidarity. Or have coffee together and listen to stories about his or her angel pin. Please do not confuse my emphasis on love as witness for anti-institutionalism. I am in deep prayer for the institutional church—but I long for a new institution to emerge from this twilight time.

Twilight is two-light. It is darkness tinged by light and light stained by darkness. The fading ember of light occupies one end of the horizon, retreating amid chaos-like defeated soldiers, while on the other end, the occupying forces of darkness are pouring in. Between the two is a confusion of light and darkness, as two opposites exist, for a few moments, in the same space at the same time. Experiencing twilight is living through a middle time. According to Lee Strobel, author of *Inside the Mind of Unchurched Harry and Mary,* only 13 percent of the American population say they still believe in all of the Ten Commandments. Mark Chaves, associate professor of sociology at the University of Arizona, says that only 28 percent of Catholics attend church on any given weekend; while fewer than one in five Protestants are in church on Sunday morning. This bothers me, since I want to get more of these people to help me support the institutional church that I love. I also believe the Holy One wants more people in worship. Anything that uses other people is outside love, Some churches are too interested in the weekly count or attendance, and witness that has an ulterior motive will not work. It will not even rebuild the institutions! But love will.

John Updike describes the marvelous decay of the Christian churches; they are "tired, grotesque, irreplaceable faiths."[1] Updike is very sophisticated in his novels and, like many believers, quite childlike in his faith. The only concrete reason he gives to support "church" is that he walked down the aisle taking collection with his father—a memory that has staying power, but one that churches have all but put to bed in him.

Too often faith is a problem for sophisticated people once they become adults. There are too many rival options to faith. Can we remain both Christian and pluralist? Can we be content with our vision of the holy and still witness to the Holy Discontents? Can we be sophisticated and simple about faith at the same time? Three alternatives are available to us.

1. We can deny the pluralist vision by affirming the truths claimed by orthodox Christianity and denying the truths claimed by other religions. We can become minimalist and relativistic. We employ these compromises in every other aspect of every experience. Why not in faith? The God we love does not insist on total obedience so much as total love.

2. We can fully adopt the pluralist vision by denying the exclusive truths claimed by orthodox Christianity. We can become anti-universalist and pro-particular.

3. We can seek a middle ground by admitting that other religions have some truth while not denying the essential truth of our own faith.

The third approach seems the most appropriate. First, however, we need to understand the greater context of Christianity's struggle with pluralism.

In *Foolishness to the Greeks: The Gospel and Western Culture* Lesslie Newbigin argues for this third position and further develops this line of thinking by saying, "we are at a point in history comparable to the one occupied by Augustine. He stood at the point where the classical vision had lost its power over people."[2] We are at that point. The way we were taught to think of religion—as universal, unchanging, eternal, and right, right, right—has estranged us from the very God we had hoped to love. There are less triumphal roads to God than some followed throughout our history. Evangelists find them. We humbly and lovingly take the back way. There, we are not sure we are right about anything concerning God. We only know how much we love God and how much God loves us and everyone else. On that firm, sure foundation, we tell anyone who will listen what we know.

Nelson Mandela expressed what he knew to be true when he spoke to the World Parliament of Religions in South Africa. He had changed his schedule to be present for the meeting. He said he did this because "religious institutions took care of the education of our children when the state abandoned them. Religious institutions made sure our children had food when we were in prison."[3] Through his words, Mandela, an agnostic, gave more witness to God's love, through embodied institutional witness, than many Christians do.

45

What we see in many holy discontents is a desperate yearning for the inner experience of the Holy. For many of them, their road to God is blocked by conceit and self-righteousness and the universalization of particular experiences—the experiences of people who seem to be so right that they are dangerous to God. These blocks are dangerous to love, not always but, nevertheless, too much of the time. Those who know God do know certainty, but they know certainty in an open, not closed, way. Genuine experience of the Holy moves to love and ethics; partial experience of the Holy is an inner high and is probably lifting a weak ego and a scared soul.

When we witness, we often begin with spirituality and end with religion. If religion is more outer, spirituality is more inner, following the guidelines Ernst Troeltsch laid out in the early part of the century. He spoke of both sects and churches being replaced by the mystic or inner focus. Ironically, it is not secularism that is the enemy of faith so much as spirituality. Spirituality, on both sides of faith, is a real enemy of love. It gets caught inside people—and they either go private and personal in their inner high, or they go public by flaunting their righteousness. Spirituality undoes the capacity for ethics and blames secularity. Spirituality is *privatized* faith. Genuine faith begins inside but moves outward, in the same way that Mandela's example described. Genuine faith becomes public love.

Pluralism has made the whole territory of the public a scary place. How dare we say anything about our faith if it has to be as small as God is love? Plus, what if we offend by saying even that? Pluralism is a real problem for witness. Sociologists differ between old style American "external pluralism," involving multiple religions within the *society,* and "internal pluralism," involving multiple religions within *individuals.* We experience the effect of both in our congregations. While we are no where near a melting pot, just as globalization has not yet wiped out all ethnicity, the trend is still leaning toward blending the populations we serve in Protestant churches.

While pluralism has made us all a bit more silent and less self-assured, both of which are good things, it need not be threatened by genuine love. Pluralism is not threatened by love, especially when that love relinquishes control and relinquishes the costumes of right and wrong. Genuine love conquers all these masquerades; genuine love humanizes people.

Elizabeth Dominguez, biblical scholar and theologian, once responded to a question on proselytization by saying, "For most people of the world they do not see the issue as one of non-Christians becoming Christians but of non-persons becoming persons."[4] Love makes persons even more concerned with becoming persons.

As someone who has responsibility for what I often call "institutional spiritual direction," I must think of persons first and Christians second. My belief is that we are already deep within the postdenominational and multifaith context and are experiencing an extensive institutional lag. We pray to gods who are too small for our people—people who live and work in different time zones, who intermarry, whose best friends are as likely to be Jewish as they are to be Muslim, and who work in a rapidly globalizing world. These people experience radical pluralism, in both their hearts and their worlds. That pluralism has to be a gift from the Creator—and as such, the Creator likes it and us. We may dare to be glad in a world of large love.

People who are "holy discontents" find some versions of God too small and others too large. They are simply not capable of wholehearted assent to parochial religion: they want and deserve more. They may retain a home in their denomination of religious origin and may also make sense of the growing constituency of people who are dismayed by any kind of religious parochialism. They can avoid "McFaith" or "Sheilaism" or, in Marva Dawn's words, "dumbed down lowest common denominator faith";[5] but these can only be avoided by refusing to make grand generalizations, other than the one about love. God's new revelation will surely be as beautiful as Bach's Lutheranism, as interesting as John Wesley's Methodism, as pure and angry as Anne Hutchinson's Puritanism, and as vital as the next Pope's Catholicism.

Poet Duncan Maclean identifies the tension of postdenominational living: we want to be safe, and we want to be free. Both are possible—but only in expanded ethical and theological frameworks that make room for the "other" in loving ways.

Sample Altar Call: Witness

We can speak boldly of God or quietly of God, especially if we make a habit of it. If we have the goal of making one act of praise or witness every day—for example, "I never would have gotten through that dark time without God" or "Isn't this an amazing opportunity that God has given us?"—then we can bide our time. We can await our opportunity. We can witness from the fullness we know by practicing the presence of God.

There may be even more strategic methods to witnessing. They need not be spontaneous. We may want to write a letter to a good friend, telling him or her what God means in our life. We may want to speak to one of our children about something important in his or her life and about how God will be with him or her. We may want to plan a retreat or time away for ourselves, especially if we feel off kilter and feel the need to "right" our boat. The point is to *plan* to witness—then follow the plan.

Chapter 4

The Importance of Small Groups

$\blacklozenge\blacklozenge$

S mall groups provide the routine experience of the safety that we gain from our experience of the Holy, which may be more rare. We speak of salvation as a profound feeling of safety. From that safety, we find the capacity to love. When and as we know salvation, we move from moral distress to moral capacity. This continuum is not a once and for all thing; like being in good physical shape, it requires frequent exercise.

Love is not always safe, as anyone who has ever loved knows. "May you love as though you have never been hurt" is a popular bumper sticker motto. Its popularity is no accident. If we are to make love the foundation of our witness to God and if we are to refrain from sneaky forms of control, it is essential that we create an experience of safety. Many Christians are dried up in our capacity to love because we do not format our intentions: we need to constantly practice the art of love. We let our strong muscles go weak. Small groups are workouts; they are exercises. They format our intentions. When love is our life practice, we often need to be picked up when we fall down and when we get hurt, which inevitably we will.

Small groups and face-to-face contact are crucial to the maintenance and sustainability of love as a response to God. In the past, pastors were able to provide the intimacy necessary for encouraging love with the pastoral call. That practice has proved unsustainable for many churches. Plus, more and more people want a less pastor-centered and a more people-centered experience in the church.

Because of the demise of pastoral calling, as well as many other equally systemic reasons, basic trust in congregations has broken down. Pastors complain about families that move away, patients who leave the hospital within hours of surgery, and genuine difficulty in gaining frequent participation in worship, church governance, and even Bible study. On the other hand, churches complain about the short tenure of many pastors: for example, in the UCC, 2.7 years is the average length of a pastorate.

The lost pattern of pastoral calling is not the only reason for the erosion of trust but it is essential enough to the knot that it deserves consideration. "Parish calling" was a small group experience; people often prayed or shared "secrets." Without that experience, or a replacement, many parishioners feel unknown in their own sanctuary.

Pastors call less than they used to because people are not home or are too busy, because pastors are more professional and desk-bound, and because people have lost the feeling that they have time just to talk. When we lose the time just to talk, we find that we are less known, know others less, and feel increasingly more isolated. Trust has a hard time developing in such a hyperactive and unreflective context.

When trust breaks down, democracy is threatened. When democracy is threatened, people fall victim to megaeconomic trends, which they imagine they are too small to control. Moral distress is the result of lost trust, lost democracy, and lost safety, and combined, these lead to vigorous knots. Small groups are a way to begin loosening the tie that moral distress has on us.

Restoring trust matters to our inner moral distress as well as our outer life in injured democracy. Even though small, face-to-face groups are a decidedly private experience, their value to public life cannot be underestimated. They are the source of our capacity to witness and love. Developing practical patterns for contact between pastor and people and between people and people is one very effective, low cost, and simple way to assist trust in growing. Small groups are an entry point into the maze and knot of moral distress.

If congregations want to sustain basic trust between pastor and people, strong encouragement of each member to participate in some small group experience is a superb first step. We can think of these small group patterns as a mutual wellness calling. Once we know the Holy, it is crucial that we experience that love with each other on a regular basis. Once a week in a Bible study or prayer group or support group or breakfast is not too much. With that regularity, we may even find ourselves surprised by a deep safety, which is fertile ground for the complexities of love.

Wellness grouping creates a contemporary culture for pastoral contact that acknowledges both the difficulties and the advantages of pastoral calling for the new century. These wellness groups distinguish between the trust that is built in crisis and the trust that is built in normal life. Using, again, Ada Maria Isasi-Diaz' concept of *lo quotidiano*, in which everyday life is understood as the site of the sacred, wellness groups intentionally place pastoral contact in both an ordinary and a sacred context. Both lay and clergy provide mutual contact and safety.

It is unnecessary to design a program for wellness groups in a church, since most of them already have a system in place through active youth, women's, men's, or Bible study groups. Regardless of the system that is used, leaders should acknowledge it and its benefits—then add on to that structure. Building an entirely new house is much less important than a good renovation. Megachurches, which have the problems attendant to their size, often require weekly participation in a randomly formed group. Mainstream churches could add these random groupings to their preexisting structures and reap many benefits.

For those who want a packaged program, Stephen Ministries, Called to Care, and Meals-on-Wheels are good places to start. Such consistent, well-trained forms of community service offer the infrastructure that love and salvation both need. In addition, members of small groups can also go bowling together or enjoy a basketball game then spend time sharing afterward. They can watch movies together, especially anything that thematically deals with the drama of redemption, like *E.T.* or *Beauty and the Beast*. Groups can read plays or books together or participate in another activity that provides a welcome respite to the modern hyperactive adult.

Your church may be ready for Discipling Groups where specific forms of commitment are made. Some small groups may be ready to graduate to high commitment situations where spiritual transformation is as much the agenda as abstaining from alcohol is for Alcoholics Anonymous (AA). Your church may prefer quarterly weekend or annual retreats. Some of these gatherings could even highlight times of silence, not all small-group activities need to require conversation. Some groups could meet in individual's homes, while others may need to be held in public places. Erma Bombeck once said that if she had her life to live over, she would have invited guests over more often even if the carpet was stained and the sofa was faded; she would have burned the pink candle sculpted like a rose before it melted in storage. She was articulating a need we all have for human contact and interaction.

Some people may initially resist the strong mission focus of these groups, but they will find that their own needs are quite well managed by the resourcing and contact that the small groups provide. According to scripture, "In the peace of Babylon, we find our own peace" (see Jeremiah 29:7). Understanding the give and take dynamic in the experience of intimacy with others is the key gift of the small group experience.

Small groups are certainly in favor of personal enrichment. But they are not just for the personal enrichment of individual lives. One important way out of moral distress is understanding "both/and" thinking. Love and salvation are neither just for us nor just for others; love and salvation are both personally enriching and world-building.

Some mainstream churches have allowed their traditional groupings to become privatized. Others only legitimate social action. As a result, too many churches have split the personal enrichment and world-building capacities that are inherent in small groups. As we renovate God's house, we might think of adding social expectations to support groups or support functions to mission groups. In any case, both kinds of groups and their mixtures must learn to pray and study the Bible together. These pieties are foundational.

Proper pastoral care is as much a foundation for active community life and institution building as it is for personal health. In churches, we care for individuals so that they may care for the world. We "restore streets to dwell in" (see Isaiah 58:12). Restored streets allow individuals to live rich, safe lives, and small groups are the church's restored streets.

According to George Gallup, 40 percent of Americans belong to small groups of one kind or another. When we employ the pattern of small groups and wellness contact in our churches, we are building on a habit that many Americans understand quite well. When we know the Holy, we are particularly open to the power of small-group work. Not only will a face-to-face involvement allow us the intimacy we need to share the joy we know; it will also discipline that joy and keep it around for as long as possible.

Many people who know the Holy well belong to large churches. Many of these large churches have learned the secret to keeping a large congregation happy. That secret is small-group involvement by large percentages of the churches' membership. In *One Another: Here for You*, Dick Meyer summarizes research from the Vital Churches Institute and relates that the membership requirement of small-group participation is rarely resisted for long, and he shows more people wanting the structure than not.

Whether the groups are affinity-based—as in women's groups or youth groups—or mixtures of people and places of friendship, small groups genuinely change people. They make lives different. In American culture, it is very hard to break out of our affinity group. We live in neighborhoods or apartments with similar mortgages or rents. We go to neighborhood schools. We socialize with those in our department, not those "above" or "below" us. Churches are one of the few places where we can break out of the cage of class or race.

Small groups are capable of diversity in a way that little else is. In small groups, we take the time to know someone who is different. We get inside their experience; they get inside ours. We are no longer strangers to one another. God's power makes us capable of finding each other over the large fences of race and class.

How do you know if your small-group experience is working to exercise the Holy in you? You have birthdays to remember. You have a place to go for the New Year. You offer hospitality. You take some aspect of faith and chew on it a bit. You have someone to catch you if you fall. You have someone to catch if they fall. Someone knows you through and through and still likes you. Someone is standing in for God and for you. Small groups give God a chance to be present to people on a regular basis. That value cannot be underestimated.

In Acts 2:42, we hear that the new disciples "devoted them-selves to the apostles' teaching and fellowship, to the breaking of bread and the prayers." Of course they did. When God touches our lives, this is what we want to do.

Sample Altar Call: Group Practice

Many women who participated in the women's movement still use a litmus test to see if they are remembering what they learned about their freedom. They see whether people participate in some form of group that constantly shapes and changes who they are as women. It is a group to which they give permission to be involved in their life as they live it.

Christians can use the same litmus test. There is no such thing as a solitary Christian. We are together the Body of Christ. We need to find a church or group to give permission to change us. Structuring church life so that such a church exists is of fundamental importance. Pastors and lay leaders need to help members find the group that meets at the right time, is made up of the right peers, and is willing to sign up for the long haul. Christians can surely change their significant group affiliations over time, and the church needs to arrange for these changes as well. No more important ministry occurs in the congregation than that of the ongoing discipling of the members.

Chapter 5

The Matter of the Meeting

◆ ◆

L eaders of churches are chief beggars: their hands hold the responsibility to feed the membership of their churches. Leaders are the elected ones, and they are the ones who hold the church's story in their heart. They are the ones to whom we go when we need to know the history of the church or get something done to turn our vision into reality. They provide comic relief when a matter gets tense, assist with a difficult problem, and encourage us when we are discouraged. They help us explore the biblical or theological insights of an issue or listen to us when we want to talk or think out loud.[1] Unfortunately, too many leaders spend too much time in meetings and not enough time in giving bread. An inquiry into the value of the meeting about the activity of beggars is long overdue. Is the meeting giving the people bread? Or stones?

Meetings imply a kind of formality and a level of resource that evangelism does not. Evangelism understands its spiritual hunger and understands its spiritual urgency. Meetings often deny hunger and live without a sense of urgency. The meeting is often all motion, with no poetry in the motion. It is often all action with no purpose. The meeting has a feeling of the ersatz about it: when we know God, we often have the opposite experience. We do not send postcards, as in the movie *Postcards from the Edge*, that say, "Having great time. Wish I was here." When we are altared by the experience of the Holy, we are having a great time *and* we are here.

My daughter recently got a new puppy. Our seven-year-old dog took one look at the puppy and said—in that way that we imagine our dogs speak—"All motion, no poetry." The little dog, Salty, snapped at the heels of the larger dog, Lilly, constantly. She ate Lilly's food, stole Lilly's toys, made herself at home in Lilly's doghouse. The day will come when these two will be inseparable, mutually useful, and fully bonded, but right now their developmental stages are mismatched. Whereas the one wants peace and quiet, the other wants action and aggravation; one wants order, the other chaos; and one wants participation, the other wants to be left alone.

Our congregations are full of these kinds of mismatches. Some people want pastors to decide everything so they can be left alone. Others want pastors to decide nearly nothing so they can participate in the decision making. The peace-and-quiet crowd and the rough-and-ready crowd have opposite desires: please one, you aggravate the other. Some people are happy with a "come what may church." They do not die if someone has forgotten to make the Advent wreath. Other people find that level of organizational chaos an affront to their spiritual order. Some people genuinely want participation. They want to sit at the table with others and fully experience the life of the parish. And others make no connection between their religious faith and the practice of democracy.

Most congregations live a *meetinged* life. Despite the fact that many members are more aesthetic in the practice of their spiritual life (that is, they want to be left alone in the practice of their faith rather than pounded together), the badge of being a church insider is the meeting. I attended a statewide gathering once and overheard lay leaders from many congregations brag about the number of church meetings they attend each month. I was abhorred. Was my faith in God and my commitment to church actually being measured by the number of nights I spent away from my family, distanced from the peace of my own solitude?

It seems to me that the puppies are winning. The organized church is more motion than poetry, more action than contemplation, more together than solitary. This hyperactivity is a significant theological failing in the churches that inherited the gospel of grace over works from the Reformation. Increasingly I see it as a practical failure as well.

There is no doubt that the meeting began to assume its throne in organizational life during the 1950s, that era of great expansion when congregations could count on extensive voluntary labor and there were multiple decisions to make about expanding resources.

People wanted church to be a site of social activity, so they constructed it that way. Now that the task of organized church life is to right-size or downsize itself, it is appropriate to ask these questions about meetings: What do we want to do with organizational authority? Does the meeting do what we want it to do? Or has it outlived its sociological usefulness? Does the old dog need to learn new tricks—or does the new dog need to learn to adjust?

More and more of our members simply do not have time for evening meetings. They may join the pastor for forty-five minutes of their lunch hour for an annual call, but they probably won't give that same time during their workday to a church-related meeting. Given the long distances people travel to work, the two-career family, and the premium placed on paid employment, surely the meeting has lost its economic ground. It is no longer supported by an abundance of volunteer time—except by a certain segment of the congregation. Theoretically, if not actually, people who are retired have enough time for those meetings, and as a result, they become quite influential in the actual life of churches, simply because they have the economic ability to participate in the way churches structure participation. In this type of structure, younger and working people become disenfranchised as a group as older adults fill more chairs around a table that a younger person cannot get to. In addition, evening meetings are especially difficult for people with children.

Conversely, congregations should be encouraging people to spend time together, in small groups that attend to God and not ersatz emergencies or Advent wreaths (that is, setting up double binds of competing goodness). For many, church versus family is the conundrum of the meeting.

Again the puppy's motion fills up the space. When I say that the church is hyperactive, I mean that activity is too much of its message. Get involved. Participate. Act. The hyperactivity is most notable in the mission field where we are exhorted to "do something" perpetually. I have become a big fan of the "don't just do something; stand there" school as I have watched mission project after mission project dwindle into measurability and three cans of soup a week. The mind and soul do not always fit the package of activity. Neither does justice fit a formula. Justice takes slow, long-term, steady, thoughtful, and prayerful action; it takes all of these and nothing less. There are other measures for mission and for participation than the do-something measure. God is not mocked by the point system in justice or salvation.

Alternately, I think of the act of witness at work. Of belonging to a labor union. Of gently correcting our parents at dinner when they make a comment that is racist or sexist. Of raising our children well. Of mentioning to our children's teacher that the vocabulary she just used about the "other" children is offensive. Of baking cookies to send to an activist who is experiencing trouble. The arts of nurture have been replaced by the arts of organization. Justice happens in daily life as well as in what we concoct at meetings.

Churches are filled with unmatched desires. Like the older dog and the younger dog, these desires have yet to make their peace with each other. Order and chaos, working and retired, happy families and avoiding families, participation and observation, poetry and motion each have a place in the life of our congregations. The worst thing about any change is the number of meetings it requires to establish it! To privilege the poetry over the motion would be as destructive for congregational life as privileging the motion over the poetry is presently. Balance is the way forward. We need ways to honor those whose participation in the church is not nightly.

We also need ways to keep meetings short enough so that people can socialize before going home, rather than filling up their notebooks with more tasks and dates and then rushing out the door. Keeping the meeting in its proper place guards the aesthetic—the poetry—that is the truly endangered species in the life of the church. Being creative, making things beautiful, observing and seeing deeply all take time. Waking up fresh to justice takes time. Keeping our imagination free for justice takes time. The aesthetic requires release from the formal agenda into the informal agenda where spirituality, not activity, is the purpose.

More and more of our people are complaining that they are not getting what they need from church: grace, acceptance, laughter, peace, genuine participation in acts of justice and imagination—the components of a healthy spirituality. Instead they get the obligations of more involvements, the tasks of fund-raising, the commandments of overwork. It is time to move the meeting off its pedestal and prepare for poetry in motion.

Why can't meetings last for one hour only and be preceded by Bible study or concluded with ice cream and apple pie? Why can't people pray for meetings or meditate in the middle of meetings if the going gets tough? Why is meeting attendance a brand of courage but not visiting the sick or those in prison? Why can't home devotions with our kids be a substitute for membership on a board or committee that meets on Tuesday nights? Why can't we imagine exercise at the gym as a mitzvah, a way to stay sane, rather than hassling one another about how to run the church?

The magnificence of the mundane lies in the company the mundane keeps. Meetings can have poetry. They can be places of division, places where the sacred catches us and snuggles us. Charles Olsen has written a wonderful manual on how to move from boards that stress activity to leaders who push spirituality; it is titled *Transforming Church Boards into Communities of Spiritual Leaders*. To avoid spending any more motion on poetry, he suggests reducing the number of people required on every committee by half or turning every other standing committee into a taskforce or honoring the people who will not go out at night, as well as those who will. The old dogs have a few tricks too. They may even know what is most important.

The good news is that many people have noticed the limitations of the meeting as an altar call—and are offering alternatives. Meetings can give bread. They do not have to give stones, but our *altared* state will have to lead us to the bread. Unfortunately, our current practice may be staler than we know. The following story may be useful as a guide to meditation since both meetings and "horse manure" grow gardens one day at a time.

The Largest Pile

On the morning of a big meeting, I found myself standing on top of the largest pile of horse manure in South Amherst, laughing my head off as I slowly made a dent in it.

I often don't go to work too early if something is happening later in the day. I want to conserve energy. By gardening, even in the winter, I find that I can keep myself alert for those low sugar hours later in the day, between four o'clock and six o'clock. This way I bite fewer people's heads off than I might otherwise.

I had been searching for a good pile of manure for snow layering since the late fall. I do not believe in growing tomatoes without an excess of horse manure. If you get in the fresh manure by January, it is delightfully ready by June planting.

For some reason, I was not finding much around. I figured I was in serious competition with the hundreds of other gardeners in my little spot in "Eden." *They* had gotten to the good stuff. *They* had already hauled it off to their own plots, and were already reaping the great benefits of manure on snow on manure on snow. The seeping of the stuff into the ground is a winter tea with high nutritional merit, according to the old folks. I always liked putting the manure on right before a snow to honor the folk wisdom.

One day I was driving along a small road south of my part of South Amherst. There was the steam. Rising straight to the sky. With that much steam, at fifteen degrees, the mother load of manure could not be far off. There it was. Almost as high as the horse barn. I careened into the driveway, almost hitting the white cat, the grey cat, and the woman mucking out the stalls—who skimmed her "shovel, flannel shirt, and horse" look out of my greedy way right at the last minute.

I asked her if I could have some. She said, "Sure." I could not have been happier.

I returned the next day to the pile, the well stacked white buckets right next to it, the manure stalls, the skittish horses, and the same mucker-out-of-stalls, the guardian of the goods, the maker of piles, and the dispenser of same.

I backed my van all the way down the long, dark, mahogany-laden horse corridor and stuck its end right up against the pile. I remarked privately how odd it was to be putting manure back into an end. But that was what I was doing, and I was delighted at the convenience. I have hauled manure longer distances.

The coincidence of my big meeting was not small. As I mounted the pile, I remembered the memos, the revised memos, the revisions of the revised memos, as well as what my political enemies were going to do this afternoon to the revisions of the revisions of the revisions. The higher I got, the deeper I got. I was in excrement twice as high as my own height. I was in excrement as wide as my house. I was in the biggest pile in South Amherst. My pride knew few boundaries. *They* didn't have this.

Then she told me. First came her flannel shirt, then her glinty shovel, then that look in her eye, so much more accustomed to manure than mine. "Get it while you can," she said. "They come tomorrow from the college to take it all."

I could have wept. I didn't. I have some self-respect left inside my own flannel shirt and behind my own shovel. I thought: How much could I haul in just one day? Even if I skipped the meeting? Three vans full? Maybe four? Could the garden take all of that? Some of this stuff was not as ripe as it could have been.

In the end, my accomplice in the tall pile showed me the best stuff: back to the north of the pile, on the far end. I took it, put it on my garden, and went on to my meeting. My laughter's source? What I knew would eventually come of all this stuff. I even had a glimpse of hope for the meeting, which was a serious contender for one of the largest piles around as well. And I could have all of the compost that I wanted from both.

Sample Altar Call: Foundation Building

Unfortunately too many churches get lost in the busy work of being a nonprofit organization; too few are actually pathways to

God. Paying attention to how meetings are conducted, how budgets are spent, how decisions are made, how staff are evaluated and supported, how lay leaders are used or abused—all of these matters are part of the intentional structuring of a church in response to the hearing of the gospel.

Many churches get lost along the way. What is important is to realize how easy it is to be found by God, how ready God is to work with us toward realignment of our organizational practice with the gospel. God's power is mighty, not small, and can de-trivialize the most driven pastor or church. Signposts include the looks on people's faces, the sense of organizational possibilities that prevail, and whether people are backbiting or supporting each other. If the negative prevails, probably something has happened to the gospel. It has "disappeared." It needs to be found. The rest will follow.

Chapter 6

The Matter of Time

◆ ◆

S aved people have enough time. Time is their air, their skin,
their own. Time to us is what water is to fish. We live in it. It is
not our enemy. It is not a commodity that we have to purchase
with time "management" techniques. Time is not an "other"; it is our
friend.

Christians have long "altared" time with the weekly observation
of a Sabbath or the daily habit of prayer. We place time on a
pedestal, and we change our relationships to accommodate it. When
the Holy enters our lives, we want even more of what Abraham
Joshua Heschel calls heavenly time, the time of the Sabbath. We
want to move from chronos time, which is marked by the clock and
the sweat of our brow, into kairos time, which, the Celtics believed,
is "thin" time touched and laced by eternity. All time is eternal—but
recognizing that all time is eternal is a Sabbath moment. That
moment can happen on the 8:15 train to Brooklyn or during the
Doxology in church.

Many of us have a large debt that we imagine we owe to time.
We will find ourselves quickly forgiven by a merciful God once we
view time as though it belonged to God and heaven, not to us.
Forgiveness—plain, old, ordinary, predictable forgiveness—is key to
time.

The biblical concept of Jubilee predicts the need for a seasonal
renewal and forgiveness. Things get out of whack predictably. The
biblical concept of the Jubilee is simply a collection of Sabbaths, or
seven years accumulated into forty-nine, with the fiftieth being the
season of putting things right.

In our normal weeks, we become discombobulated. Things pile
up. The coffee table joins the counter in becoming the home of

unopened mail, unpaid bills, scarves worn once and discarded, and old newspapers. On Sabbath we clean our spiritual house. We unclutter. We start over. We regroup. These simple patterns of living, and then putting away our living, are the basis of Sabbath-keeping. They are also the basis of death and resurrection as Jesus knew it. We go to a prepared place. We imitate Jesus' preparation of place by preparing our own. The prepared place is a mansion; it is many rooms. It is ample. It is spacious. And it is uncluttered.

One summer my husband lost a ring I had given him. It was a ring with three small diamonds in it, reminding him of each of our three children. He caught a mean fly ball during an adult softball game and jammed his ring finger, thus necessitating the removal of the ring. He put it in his pocket. Or so he thought. The ring never showed up, even though we have wasted lots of time looking for it.

The ring has a Sabbath to it: every time we tell the story of the lost diamonds, we remember our love for each other. We recite it. We ritualize it. The ring is gone in the same way that the corn was eaten by the hungry man. (Remember the pharisees trying to trick Jesus into rules for the Sabbath: "Can corn be picked on the Sabbath?" [see Matthew 12:1-8.]) Sometimes we do things that we "shouldn't" really do. We get out of whack so regularly that Sabbath has to come as a reminder—a remembrance of whose we are. In keeping Sabbath and opening time to eternity, we remember what life points to rather than what it is now.

The ring points to my husband's and my love. The corn pointed to the Sabbath law. But Sabbath is something beyond itself. It is time for God, and God is more than rules, more than diamonds. Keeping Sabbath is something we try to do more than something we actually do.

First World people have much to repent; we have much changing to do. We have spent long periods dishonoring time. Our discombobulation is not just personal: it is also social and political and economic. Why do we dishonor time by "otherizing" it and using it and managing it? Because we understand our cultural marching orders to accumulate and move upward. It takes time, abused time, to fulfill these orders.

Too many of us are obeying these orders way too much.

Interestingly, the Jubilee movement to cancel world debt is a large forgiveness; it incorporates our need for forgiveness into the justice of forgiving the world debt. Nevertheless, we cannot simply cancel—out of some privileged largess—Third World debt. We, too, must change. We need to get beyond what Barbara Brown Taylor calls real crimes of first-degree guilt and second-degree anxiety.

Many middle-class Americans do not understand forgiveness because we do not understand sin; we feel as though we have never done anything "big" wrong and, therefore, do not need or understand the refreshment of forgiveness. We also feel helpless about justice for the larger world—and we sin more with that helplessness and hopelessness than in any other way. Our sins are hidden even from ourselves! But starving children know them very well.

In the keeping of the Sabbath, in the welcoming of a personal jubilee, we repent the sin of hopelessness. We get back into our water. Hope allows us to stop hiding from our sins and enables a capacity to connect to the poor and the strangers, those we now fear but could love. In Sabbath and personal jubilee, we see how our fate is connected to the fate of those whose faces we do not see—and how blocking them is blocking our deeper selves out too. We are all God's people. Saved people cannot forget this spiritual fact.

The benefits of keeping Sabbath come by regularizing and patterning our contact with God. You can keep the Sabbath on Sunday, Saturday, or every morning—or any way you want to keep it. Likewise with Jubilee: you do not have to be fifty years old or in a millennial moment to want to observe it. You can reorient your relationship to time, through forgiveness, in a ritualized Sabbath or in a special Sabbath. God continuously stands ready to live with us in time and eternity. Keeping Sabbath, *altaring* our relationship to time, is an obvious response to the Holy in our lives. We do not necessarily become radically different, but we definitely become different.

If, indeed, there is not something big we can do to change the world, are there small things we can do? What is enough? How do we know? Are there ways to pay off the debt of hopelessness with hope? Or does God cancel that debt in us? How? We do not even get close to these kinds of questions if we cannot find the time to keep Sabbath. When we find the time, God offers us these questions—and even some answers.

Keeping Sabbath often offers small answers to huge questions. We know the grace of God in Sabbath-keeping and no longer set ourselves up to fail. Instead of saving the entire world, we can befriend one "faceless" person and pray for them. Or we can be a part—not a huge part, just a proportionate part—of our local community organization. Keeping Sabbath is as much about getting our pain out of the world's pain as anything. In God's time, we get ourselves off the center point and on to God's centering points.

When we live in God-centered time, and off self-centered time, we experience things differently. Road rage, shame about our own credit card debt, or irritation at being put on hold for hours by our health care provider are different experiences for people who have some comfort and center somewhere.

Many of us get bent out of shape by the little stuff. The reason is often that there is no place for the big stuff in our life. Sabbath-keeping makes space for the big stuff. It reminds us of the difference between the large and the small.

Why do we not live with consistent genuine personal authority? We are the Body of Christ. We are created in the image of God. All have sinned and fallen short of the *glory of God*. That glory is our intended place. Why do so many people and so many situations intimidate us? Why do the little things people say against us bother us so? What are we really afraid of—dying without living, perhaps, or having to go on alone, without the approval of our intimates?

Saved people remember what God has said about and to us more than what our detractors have said. Saved people memorize scriptures and repeat them when people insult us. Saved people refuse to treat others as badly as they treat us. Saved people take the time to remember whose they are.

People who do not keep Sabbath have insulted God and God's love for them. That is not a small sin. That is an ontological sin, violating creation and its seventh day of rest. It is the sin of indifference, of not believing what our loving parent has told us is true.

Sabbath-keeping is based in the great commandment that we love God and our neighbor as we love ourselves. The Golden Rule and the Paternoster are the basis for our relationship with God. What does that line, "forgive us our debts as we forgive our debtors," mean? What is the connection between our repentance and our ability to forgive others? What if we think we cannot repent? Can God still forgive our debt to God?

Yes. This is what saved people discover when we keep the Sabbath, when we move into God's mansion of time. We believe that God will triumph in human history, physically and spiritually, and live as though that promise were already true. We refuse to doubt the activity or power of God. We forgive the debts owed us as a sign that we believe God will forgive us. We forgive injuries as soon as possible—and live forward, not backward.

Jubilee forgiveness is what we know in small ways every time we keep a Sabbath and separate our kind of time from God's time. Sabbath is that separation; it is the awareness that God's time is what really matters. Jubilee forgiveness, the second chance, the chance to reorder, is what Jesus meant by "seventy times seven" as the number of times we should forgive each other. God offers that infinite amount of opportunities to reenter time, to live again in a new way. Jubilee forgiveness connects the pattern of forgiveness to the pattern of Exodus, in which the Israelites leave Egypt, cross Jordan, and come into Jerusalem. There is an Exodus pattern and cycle to forgiveness. A friend has written a novel with the provocative title *The Portable Egypt*. We move in and out of Egypt all the time!

Sabbath-keeping recognizes the circle of forgiveness, from wronging or being wronged, to repentance, to grace, to new behavior, and back to wronging and being wronged. It is this circle and cycle that Jesus refers to with seven times seven; this perpetual spiral of forgiveness is personal jubilee. Jubilee is the experience of the Israelites after the Exodus. Jubilee is what we do when we have made a historical mess of things, and we need to right history, personally and politically.

The Sabbath cycle yields continual forgiveness and renewal. It is a positive, life-giving spiral whereas the absence of forgiveness is encouragement to further sinning, even across the generations. The forgiven place is a place that stops the wounding of ourselves, one another, and future generations. The forgiven place is the eternity that we want. And which God fully intends and will bring about.

In keeping Sabbath we get up nine times for every eight times we fall down or slip back into our old ways. We live the seventy-times-seven promise. Sabbath-keepers are deeply aware of the connections between spiritual and economic experience; we no longer separate them. Nor do we have additional need to separate the rich from the poor.

Religious and economic principles rarely converge as well as they do in the growing movement for global debt resolution, known widely as Jubilee 2000. The fundamental Christian principle of forgiveness for sins joins an uncannily practical movement to save the world's economy by canceling the unpayable debts of poor nations. Forgive us our debts, we pray, as we forgive our debtors: we usually mean this line from the Paternoster spiritually. The Jubilee movement asks us to join a material prayer to the spiritual prayer.

This coincidence of the economic and the spiritual is not uncommon in Christian faith. Easter is dangerously misinterpreted by many as a strictly spiritual experience. When we speak of victory over death, surely there is no such victory if people who are spiritually uplifted remain physically beaten down. If Jesus were to rise today, would he rise in the movement for global debt resolution? His resurrection would forgives debt so that Ugandans might pay seventeen dollars a person on health care and three dollars a person on foreign debt instead of the exact opposite, which they do at present.

Christian faith is material and spiritual freedom simultaneously. The beloved hymn "Rock of Ages" was composed out of economic experience, rather than spiritual experience. Thomas Hastings wrote the tune to which it is usually sung, and Augustus Toplady published all four stanzas for the first time in 1776 to compare the burden of English national debt to the burden of sin. Rock was offered as a solace to both real sin and real debt.

New life is very real to those who know the cancellation of debt. Visit Alcoholics Anonymous (AA) any night of the week, in any community in America. You will hear the stories of canceled debts. These debts are not imagined; they are real. So is the resurrection.

The Resurrection of Jesus is connected to Israel's Year of Jubilee as a practical solution to the sins of the world. Every seven years, the land would be redistributed. Jubilee frees hopelessly indebted people the same way bankruptcy frees an individual. It creates new land and new time. Freeing hopelessly indebted countries from all debt without condition is what Jesus has done by his death on the cross. Debt is canceled in new life. Debt is not personal sin. Most debt was contracted by authoritarian or military regimes: the people now paying the debt did not sign up for their monthly fees. They should not be responsible for the debt they cannot pay at any rate. Restructuring Third World debt could turn the world from death to life, overnight. Resurrection could be measured out in the teaspoons of percentage points, nation by nation. In personal jubilee, we measure out our lost anxiety and renewed confidence in similar small amounts. The following story may help illustrate this point.

One night two worlds collided as I was studying the text for my Sunday preaching, a text from Samuel about what to do with the stranger and the foreigner. We had yet another horrible car crash in front of our house on the road that connects Amherst and Holyoke. We know the thud well since this is a bad road—twenty people have died on the road in the last three decades. Somebody new had lost the direction of the road; it is easy to think the road turns in front of our house. We ran out to see how bad it was this time, with one of the adults guarding the children because their eyes are too used to the carnage already. It was my husband's turn to stay with the kids.

This time a very pregnant woman stumbled out of the front seat of a black car holding a one-year-old child. The driver, a man, came out of the other side. Both were speaking softly to each other in Spanish, their language of origin, the language of Holyoke. The child was screaming. The front of the car was totally bashed in. They were very lucky to be alive.

Across the street a white van was burning. The English-speaking man ran across the street to the Spanish-speaking man, yelling, "Who is going to pay for the damage!" He did not ask about the child. He did not ask about the pregnant woman. He simply screamed, "Who is going to pay for the damage!"

I had called 911 on my way out of the house. The police were arriving just in time to see this exchange. An older policeman arrived and took a minute to see if the child was all right. Then the policeman asked for licenses—although he never did look at the license of the man with the white car, the damage concern, and the English accent. Within seconds, the driver of the black car was up against the cruiser with his hands in the air. (I wish the cars had not been black and white; they were.) The driver of the black car did not have a license. He was handcuffed, put in the back of the cruiser and taken to jail. As it turned out, he had just gotten out of jail that morning—for driving without a license. He was in big trouble. What did Samuel say again? "When the foreigner comes into your country listen, hear. See."

The pregnant mother and bawling child were left standing in the street, next to someone's totaled black car, which was being towed away. The child's pacifier was towed away with the totaled car. The child was inconsolable.

I had a car that worked, so I jumped into it to go to the drugstore to get a replacement pacifier. When I got to the drugstore to get a pacifier, it was closed, but there was another young woman there also desperate for some purchase. She looked like the poster girl for a facial cosmetic. (I called her "Noxema girl" in my mind.) She was a student of some kind. I asked her if she would go to the twenty-four-hour grocery; when she got her item, she could also go get a pacifier. I would go to the jail and sit with the mother and child. I shoved three dollars in her hand and told her some of the story. She answered me with an all-American and rather cheery, "Aye, aye, Captain." She went to the grocery, returned very quickly to the police station, gave the baby the pacifier, and returned my three dollars to me.

What the girl did was a little thing. So little it dare not register on the Richter scale of human kindness. But she showed an eagerness to be connected with the suffering of the world, to give real bread, or something, to the children. That eagerness is the one Samuel commanded in his admonition, "listen." We want to connect. We want to hear. We want to hear above and below the thud of collision of the worlds. We want to say "Aye, aye" to the right captain.

The white man was not all wrong; he was in his own prison, but he was not all wrong. Undoubtedly the international question is, Who is going to pay for the damages? It is the American's question at the table. It is ours. We can be as ashamed of it as we want, but it is our question. An unlicensed, undocumented, unpaid for vehicle with no collateral has run off the road and hit our nice car. If it has not happened, if your neighborhood is still safe from these sorts of things, good for you. It cannot be safe forever.

We know the gospel answer to these damages. It is that we are going to pay for them. We will pay for the damages the more Jesus Christ grows in our hearts. The more he grows the more we will be able to pay. The less we love our vans, the more we will love our children—and "their" children. We will buy pacifiers and not ask for reimbursement. We will hear the countries that want to be heard from and not be afraid or unable to hear the depth of what they have to say. They are in jail. They cannot afford good cars. They are going to drive anyway.

Paying for the damages is really the least of our wealthy country's problems. The greater problem is the way we ask that question when our white van is hurt. Why do we care so much about the wrong thing? What about the screaming child, the pregnant mother, and the lack of options for the man who already had no license? Why did the cop not take the license of the man driving the van and at least look at it? Why did a white cop in a liberal, Massachusetts college town throw the Spanish-speaking man up against his cruiser and never lay a hand on the white man, who was being obscene in his reaction to the accident? The other man had lost a lot; he had lost only a little, but he only cared about the little he lost. Why? Is that kind of greed not a larger problem than payment for the damages? Is it not damage itself?

Damaged is the word to describe the spirit of the First World; people in the First World are often called soulless by those with significantly less material wealth. Damage is what happens to our days when we do not do simple things like keep the Sabbath. We lose our good time and get bad time, polluted time. We waste the days of our breath and life.

How can we repair these damages so that we can be the people we were meant to be? How can we be the people we want to be, with an "aye, aye" coming out of our beautiful complexions to the right captain? Could a little do a lot? Could personal jubilee be three dollars on a regular basis? Without such personal jubilee, is there any reason to hope that the cancellation of global debt will change the world the way God wants the world to change? Isn't scripture clear about the inner turning coming before the outer turning? Inner transformation and conversion almost always precede outer transformation.

To get ready for Jubilee 2000, we may have to comfort the women and the children who get stranded on the road. Our hearts may have to open to them—and worry less about how to pay for the damage done by them. We may have to keep Sabbath to achieve the capacity to really see what is going on.

As I write, the radio tells a story of an Albanian crossing the border into Macedonia. She walked sixteen hours across the mountains; she went into labor when she arrived on the border, and there—with NATO bombings overhead and thousands of people, heading nowhere, having been driven from their homes, in line with her—her child was born. Mary, the mother of Jesus, understood. We can too. Little things, little attentions, will do as a start: Listen. See. Hear. The strangers are right outside our door, on our roads, in our towns. We are the strangers as much as they. We are strangers to ourselves, strangers to each other, strangers to our own capacity to be Christlike in compassion. Our damage needs to be paid for. God will pay for us in the same way that God will free the poor nations from demoralizing debt. We cannot pay either. But God can.

I cannot replace the ozone that the separation of my spiritual and physical worlds has cost. I cannot keep guns out of little kids' hands. I cannot even find the man who went to jail that night—but I still have his wife's earring. She left it on the couch. What I can do, because God has freed me and canceled my debts, is listen to and see and hear the people in my front yard and beyond. I can hear the cry of God's people because I am free to hear it. I can use my time to hear it.

God makes us whole even after we are broken. God finds us even after we have long been lost. God puts together what is broken asunder. All of us know what it means to be separated from our true self.

One forty-year-old man described his life as "having missed every train I should have caught." He may be quite wrong in that assessment of what his life "should have" been, but there is no doubt that he lives a deep disappointment. He lives a longing for a past he did not have. He can be saved by imagining a different future, a jubilee time. He can practice the wisdom of that great bumper sticker motto, "It is never too late to have a happy childhood." No debt is too large.

Most of us know the world is not itself yet. We have not found each other. We have missed the train we should have caught. The train is justice; the obstacle is our fear to love. The obstacle is our "compassion fatigue," or that time when we are tired of caring— even when we have not actually stretched ourselves.

Rather than living double binded between the rock of justice and the hard place of fear, imagining a Jubilee that could let us slip out of our tomb. Keeping the Sabbath regularly is the first step toward new life. We have enough time.

Sample Altar Call: Keep Sabbath

People who know God are able to rest. Sabbath used to mean Sunday for Christians and Saturday for Jews. It was the day taken off from work for God—and for the rest that religion brought to people who took regular Sabbaths. On the seventh day, we imitated God. We did not work or even create. We took time for time: time for God, first, and then time for each other and ourselves came along as part of the bargain. Recentered, we find our way to each other and to ourselves. We find that way through God.

Sabbath is as much what it is not as what it is. Sabbath empties us without taking from outside of ourselves. It is not television or television's dramatic replacement of our story with someone else's story. It is not "blitzing out." It is not hiking, with its grand viewpoints and heavy breathing and body-changing, feel-good potential. Nor is Sabbath time to do errands, get caught up on our desk stress, pay our bills, or visit our relatives.

Sabbath means a larger relief. It is a time in God, for God. It is more like the kind of vacation people mean when they say, "I'm so tired that even a month's vacation won't do." Sabbath is religious rest. It is time for play, taken from time dedicated for work.

Observance of Sabbath and its separation of time into work and play paradoxically unifies our time. It makes it all ours. We find the goodness and Godness—the for-itself-ness—of "our" time. Sabbath is both the seventh day dedicated to God and rest and any other time we take for God and rest. Sabbath can self-empty any time, any way. How do we begin to move God back into the house that God has been exiled from by time abuse? By observing Sabbath. By emptying ourselves so there is room for God, from time to time.

Chapter 7

The Confidence of Knowing the Basics of Our Faith

◆ ◆

A Three Part Course

Saved people know their tradition. Salvation is a simultaneously intellectual, spiritual, economic, and physical experience. It works on all burners, including those of the traditions of the faith. We know some things so well we do not know them at all. Many of us last studied Christianity when we were children in Sunday school. Much of our embarrassment at the act of witness comes from fear of being children, of being outed for having what Jesus treasured as a childlike faith. While Christians are childlike in our faith, we are also adults in it. Adults need to know what they think about the basics and be able to emerge the submerged in order to get a fresh look at some of the basics of our faith. Such topics as *biblical authority*, *Golden Rule*, and the *Ten Commandments* are considered basic.

A good attitude for adult Christian education leaders to have is to make believe they are putting on a different pair of glasses, making things look different as a result. Some matters will be larger, some smaller. Some you may not ever have seen before—like the stain on my good jacket the dry cleaner saw, causing her to refuse to try to clean it. I had been unaware of the stain and had been wearing it for weeks. Embarrassment is already my intimate companion; thus, my willingness to talk about theology in this basic way! The eyeglasses can view large areas like:

- God: The Creator
- Jesus: The Redeemer

- The Holy Spirit: The living, present part of God
- The Trinity: How these three persons of God interrelate
- Scripture: The stories and memories of God
- Sin: The way we go wrong or get estranged from God
- Eschatology: Where things are going

Our method will be to look at each of the three basic topics (biblical authority, the Golden Rule, and the Ten Commandments) from the perspective of each of these sets of glasses. We could also look at each of these glasses from another of the sets of glasses, and we could even take the three basic subjects and look at the glasses. The possibilities are endless. For these three sessions, however, we will content ourselves with a seven on three approach—which has a certain biblical ring to it anyway.

We will go to these three versions of theological embarrassment, in a safe environment, where no one will laugh at what we do not know or cannot see. From the embarrassment, we will emerge to a simple light, the light of "theology," and not be afraid, any longer, of its potential insults about our limited sight.

Theology is simply what we know about God (*Theo*: God; *logy*: knowledge). And there is nothing simple about that! Lots of people know lots about God from many sources. A child who is dying of leukemia has an *experience* of God greeting her on the other side after she or he dies. A pastor has an experience of God because he or she has *studied* theology. A layman may read a section of *scripture* every night and may have learned how present God can be in word and promise and story. One person may have been having a bad day from his or her arthritis on communion Sunday and gotten to church anyway because he or she wanted a *eucharistic* experience of God. Still, another person may have had a direct *revelation,* where God may have spoken in a dream about something large or small. Each of these (experience, study, scripture, communion, revelation, and church fathers and mothers) and more are sources of knowledge about God. In the beginning of our little tutorial, we will want to know which of these several authorities tell you who God is. If you are like most people, you are "right-handed" with some and "left-handed" with others. In other words, experience might come easy to you but scripture does not, or vice versa.

Remain humble! A lifetime and five university degrees would not be enough to actually learn theology. There are too many languages to know, too many layers to remove, too much that is stunning that has already been said. Yet, you and I live on the top of this enormous mountain of knowing and seeking now—with the same limitations of those in C.E. 400, 800, or 1200. We can only know what our generation can know, not more or less. We can choose ongoing embarrassment at how little we know or, with the Hubble telescope, we can gaze in awe at what there is. Limited awe. Embarrassed awe. Humble awe. That awe will be the permission we give ourselves to take a quick look at theology—hoping for a Hubble but knowing we just have some reading glasses from the local drugstore. They, and God's wish that we know God, will have to suffice. Our sense of the small and limited is probably the best approach to theology that can be made. God, after all, chose Bethlehem and not Jerusalem to make a stand! I think of this chapter as something that should be done slowly, over three sessions. You may think there is a better way to do it!

Session One

The Authority to Know God

We can know God by tradition. Or experience. Or reason. Or all three. Or some other way. I prefer the combination and the blend. That is why I, who love Jesus the Christ, married a Jew, who doubts that Jesus is Christ. His religious authorities and mine often engage in personal warfare. I may say that everything is going to turn out all right, and he may say the same thing, but rarely do we say the same thing at the same time. My faith is often based in the future, his in the past. My hope is often based in a serious, death dueling transformation; his is often based in becoming more stationary, more obedient. His faith is often based in what I see as stubborn rigidity; mine in what he sees as flighty fluidity.

I call these civil wars "the battle of the worldviews." He insists I am overly pessimistic and (his favorite word) "apocalyptic." I insist that he is overly pessimistic and "cynical." I do not see his hope; he does not see mine. I see his hope as insufficiently strong to wage war with my despair. He sees mine the same way. If Jesus did not die on the cross and rise on the third day, of course, he would see my transforming pushes as unreliable. My favorite definition of the gospel is that it is the permission and commandment to enter difficulty with hope, borrowed from the Canadian theologian, Douglas Hall. We go into a kind of tomb. We come out of a kind of tomb. That is how hope works. It works by transformation.

My husband's hope is much less dialectical and less fluid. For him, what we do is get deeper onto the band of God's historical activity. We move from disobedience to obedience. We become more ourselves or more our "better" selves. I often do not have the energy for that self-centering in history righteousness. He rarely has the courage of the tomb. Of course, we surprise each other. I have seen him transform overnight in response to a suggestion by a doctor; I have stuck on a bead so hard that it is he who prays that great prayer "pry her off dead center." Still, the authorities and the way we know God are fundamentally different.

Similarly, some Americans are convinced that since the Bible does not teach evolution, schools should not teach it either. This argument about authority reduces authority to the canon, that one scripture which is understood as eternal. Only books written long ago are genuinely scriptural, thus locking God into one or another time period. Do not worry: God bursts out.

In battles between Jews and Christians, for example, there is the additional burden of there being two testaments, a first and a second, what many call the Old and the New, implying what many Christians believe is the fulfillment of the first by the second through Jesus.

Literal interpretations of scripture are ironically hard on biblical authority, if for no other reason than we cannot eat pork, must wear hats, and other historical equivalents. Unfortunately, God is active in history, according to the doctrine (a formal belief put together over time by groups of people who have really thought about it) of the Trinity. God did not stop with creation, or even with Jesus, but stays on in the Holy Spirit, who is as good as God and Jesus, who are both as good as the Holy Spirit. The Holy Spirit opens time for Jesus and God.

In obedience to the doctrine of the Trinity, we become religious open-endedness—right at any given moment, but not completely right. This open-endedness, this lack of a closed universe, this rubbed raw door at the bottom of our heart, becomes our religious authority. It is not relativism—because what happens in our encounter with God is not relativism at all. It is instead the nearly constant and flawed move to win points for your side, to show the virtue and benefit of transformation over continuity, for example. We fight for these things because we believe in them. We fight intimately, not on a soapbox. The opening in our heart, our cosmos, our worldview gets rubbed raw—and it also lets in the wind. It scabs over from time to time only to get rubbed raw again. As Wendell Berry says about marriage itself, marriage is the willingness to get lost in the forest and the necessity to go out into the clearing again. Even after you have become afraid of the light.

This open place in the bottom of us is the place where the Holy Spirit indwells. God, without whom nothing is, and in whom we live and move and have our very being, gave us the Holy Spirit on purpose. The Holy Spirit is not God's rival but God's agent.

A minister in New York City tells a joke about his father riding an airplane. "Do you really believe this thing can fly and hold you up?" "I'll tell you the truth, Son, I never did put all my weight down on that plane." When religious authorities war intimately, we become blessedly and mercifully incapable of putting all our weight down on our own certitude.

Downeast Mainers tell us that if you want to sink fast you should hang on to the anchor. And that is how I feel about my Christ. I never thought Jesus would want me to hang on too tight. That is the gospel I hear from him consistently. We can have what we can let go of. We can be rich if we can be poor. We give to get. We lose our life to gain it. We relinquish, not hold. Thus, my very absolute faith in letting go and being open, in not putting my weight down too fully anywhere. The gospel, in my little kernel of it, is the freedom to float. And float, I do.

In my experience, change is inevitable, but growth is optional. Like many other people, I have noticed that what used to be called the certainty of the components of the atom are no longer so at all. These things are, furthermore, not a still or fixed point but rather a motion, a bit like how I imagine the Trinity—an interrelationship of moving matter. Why would I need the authority of a fixed God? Would that not be blaspheming the atom and the Golden Rule, simultaneously? The authority of my religious experience is an experienced place, which is in dialogue with reason, scripture, and the church parents.

The authority is the knowledge that the One who made us will bring us home. That the Creator God is in charge of the destination of both me and the world. Creation and Eschatology—the sense of the end, the intended end from the beginning, the Omega, the Alpha birthed—are linked by religious authority as open-endedness.

Sin is missing the mark of this open creation; sin is becoming estranged from God's origination and destination for us. Sin is the refusal to become what we are intended as children of God. Sin is getting lost on the way from Alpha to Omega.

I call this place of authority the wounded door, or opening, or crack where the air and light comes. That wounded door is the religious authority of me confronting the other and myself, simultaneously. At that nexus or node, I experience Jesus and who and the way he was. What amazes me about Jesus is that he is God incarnate, come down to be here, in human form. Jesus is the ideal human, or the human face of God. Did he transcend his humanity? Absolutely. Can I? Probably not. But I can be raised from the dead by keeping my inner door open to the experience, through the Holy Spirit, of the word of God in Jesus. Word made flesh and living among us, which is a nice trinitarian formula itself.

These individual images and certitudes are also in dialogue with the church, both ancient and experienced. That dialogue is often painful for someone like me, who is right-handed with inner personal authority and left-handed with outer, communal authority. The church is often another word for church fathers. It is, according to scripture, the very body of Christ, but for me, it has been more the body of the church fathers. The rather dead body, actually.

I am willing to look at religious authority *in* the church, but I am not as willing as I might be to look at religious authority *as* the church. I believe the Trinity is my warrant for finding God in parking lots as well as cathedrals. New revelations are needed. I have no problem looking for them in the parking lot, or in the eyes of my puzzled Jewish husband. I have this urge to look "elsewhere" for God rather than rounding up the usual suspects. That urge is an urge for authority. It is something that feels deeper than even magnificent African American worship or great table prayers, each of which are sites where I can usually count on God. When I rush to the openings, I am looking not just for God but for more God, for deeper God, for God eternal.

I know God because I am an escape artist. I work the raw openings. Most people find this kind of flexibility infuriating. For me, it gives permission to skip out of services. My faith is in the hallway as much as the sanctuary. My fluidity is directly related to the fundamentalism of my youth. It grounded me enough to fly. Fundamentalism gave me religious ground, religious equity. From there, I have religious experience.

Religious authority comes from reason and experience and tradition. Reasoning through my experience as I stand in left field and my best friend stands in right has often brought me to God. Surely religious institutions have also brought me to God. I have asked God more than once how long I have to stay in the institutional church that drives me crazy. The answer has this odd ring. "Seventy times seven." It is the same answer Jesus gave when asked how often we have to forgive our neighbor. I am stuck, in the church, standing at its door. I am stuck in an interfaith marriage, waving at my partner from right to left. There is no center field in this game. God comes in experience at the open door. God comes as we pass through, waving.

An interesting exercise to do as you seek your own religious authority is to read Mary Belenky's *Women's Ways of Knowing*. In it we are given a typology that instructs people to move from a place of silence and voicelessness to a place where they are willing to receive external authority, on to a place of subjective authority in which the self is authority but a person is still distrustful of external authorities and experts. The goal in the somewhat hierarchical typology is to get to a place of connected and constructed methods of knowing, a place in which authority, ideas, and power are shared, where one has a sense of personal authority as well as respect for external authorities.

Session Two

The Ten Commandments

In this session we will look at one of the pillars of faith for most Christians, the Ten Commandments. We will see how God, Jesus, and Holy Spirit are represented and what they say to us about sin, eschatology, and the Trinity. The Trinity is widely understood as beginning in the Creation, with God's full plan and origination. Is there a Christ—or, watch the big word, *Christology*—in the commandments? If not, why not?

Let's focus our discussion on the question of whether the Commandments should be taught in the schools. But first, tell someone close to you in your own words what they mean to you. Notice their reaction when you bring up the subject. Have a serious conversation about whether we should publish them in public schools. If it would do no harm to publish the Ten Commandments in public schools, then those who love them would not need to worry about the initial decision to make such publication possible. Because such publication will do harm, those who love the "ten words" (as the Hebrew reads) are compelled to oppose it.

The harm is in the trivialization of what is profound. The harm is in the clumsy intervention of the state in society. The harm is in making the terribly difficult task of moral living appear simple. These hypocrisies cannot help but do harm to a youth that increasingly refers to adults as "clueless." If adults want children to honor their father and mother, then honorable actions are required.

The Ten Commandments are widely understood by Jews and Christians as a profound literary and religious document. Some proponents anxiously worry that people do not know what the Commandments are or where to find them. They are found in the book of Exodus, which is the second book in the Bible, in chapter 20, verses 1-14.

The numbering of the ten differs slightly in the Jewish and Christian traditions. Jewish tradition separates those Commandments that address the relationship between God and human beings, the first few, from those that involve human society alone, the remainder. The Commandments say ten things in differing degrees of shorthand. There are dozens of Bible translations, each of which has to take a stand on the correct phrasing for the ten words. Do not be surprised if the version you memorized or read is different from mine! Or if its order or enumeration differs.

One of the problems the public schools will face is the question of which version should be posted—not an unimportant problem. Those who love the Bible have been quarreling for years about the accurate translations; that quarrel is an important one, filled with genuine religious significance. It might be the kind of thing our teachers could teach in the schools because it would carry the spirit of the Commandments, rather than their letter to the students. This is the version I know by heart:

- Thou shalt have no other gods before me.
- Thou shalt not bow down before idols.
- Thou shalt remember the name of God to keep it holy.
- Remember the Sabbath day to keep it holy.
- Honor your father and mother.
- Thou shalt not kill.
- Thou shalt not commit adultery.
- Thou shalt not steal.
- Thou shalt not bear false witness against thy neighbor.
- Thou shalt not covet (followed by a long list of things we are not to covet).

Interestingly, Jesus, millennia following Moses, says that the Ten Commandments boil down to what we now refer to as the "Golden Rule," which is also widely misinterpreted as meaning "do unto others what you would have them do unto you." The Golden Rule is actually to love God first and your neighbor as yourself. In each instance of general misinterpretation, the God part is made horizontal. God is what we forget. This same amnesia curses the religious wrong or right. God would never post commandments in a public hall. The act itself is beneath God.

What could we do with the commandments to protect them and keep them sacred? At one time, people memorized them. However, memorization has acquired a bad name—having been abused by more than one public or religious school teacher—so very few of us now know things by heart. An interesting exercise might be to repeat the Commandments by heart. If adults could recite something from memory and from the heart to children, that would probably do a great deal of good for public and private relations for the Decalogue, or ten words. Anything less genuine than saying them from the heart—as in posting them—does harm to their very holiness.

Imagine congress passing a law that says: all adults should memorize the Ten Commandments and recite them before they get a driver's license. We would be taking beauty and turning it into regulation. Odd, isn't it that those who oppose most forms of regulation are often too willing to regulate and diminish religion?

Why do we treat youth as needing regulation? And ourselves as needing hands-off, legalized coveting? The answer is hypocrisy. Thou shalt not commit hypocrisy. Learn it by heart. Saved people know what God wants in their heart. That is the mark of an *altared* person.

Session Three

The Golden Rule

Jesus does an amazing thing when he "unseats" the religious authority of the Ten Commandments on behalf of one rule, now called the Golden Rule, which says we are to love God first and our neighbor as ourself. Of the many things that he says in the four Gospels, this message about loving God first and loving our neighbor as ourself is widely understood as original and seminal with Jesus.

This Golden Rule certainly simplifies the issues raised by the Commandments in session two. But often it gets "horizontalized" by our horizontal society. Often it comes to mean treatment for the neighbor, and in a crude "functional atheism"—meaning we speak of God spiritually, but we dismiss God from our days, our datebooks, our checkbooks, and so on—we forget about God altogether. Kathleen Norris, the writer of *Dakota* and many other books, claims to understand almost everything about Christianity except Christ, and Christianity without Christ left an emptiness, a void, at the center of her belief.[1] Her experience of the "horizontal" Christian is one many share.

Norris does a study of faith in *Amazing Grace*. She goes digging for the God she is to love first and most of all. She employs the image of the quark, an elemental particle, to explain her understanding of the Trinity. Only quarks could show us the dance of communal interrelationship at the heart of God. Norris says that it was Tertullian who brought her religious energy into the outer planetary rings of trinitarian faith. The image is that of the Trinity as a plant, with the Father as a deep root, the Son as the shoot that breaks forth into the world, and the Spirit as the beauty and fragrance that is spread throughout.

Oddly, in this image she goes back to the same dynamism that Augustine said was at the heart of the Trinity, at the heart of the kind of God we are to love. Our God is one of fundamental, original relationship, even within the self of God. Norris appreciates those who live outside relationship with this God, the so-called unchurched. She recounts the story of a preacher who tries to get a deal from a delicatessen owner. He orders the plate lunch in the name of the "unchurched." At the center of the plate when it comes is bologna in the shape of a cross.[2]

Norris is a good example of a pre-Christian, one who is trying to live simply and well. She joins many Americans in valuing the Golden Rule: they may not be religious, but they try to follow the Golden Rule.[3] Oddly, for Jesus that Golden-Ruled life would be fully trinitarian, dynamic, *in* the church if not *of* the church. For Jesus, God is the one who centers all the rest; relationship to God is what matters.

The Golden Rule often seems vanilla in flavor when people first hear it. "You certainly can't go wrong there," they think. Well, watch out! Christians who obey the Golden Rule and put God in the center of their life are able to keep on going, through the great freedom of this nation to its great community. They are able to walk the beatitude walk, the paradox walk, to run the race long enough to see defeat through to victory. The victory God wants. The victory God wrote in the DNA of creation and history at the beginning of time.

Duncan Maclean has described his faith as a noose, but one that keeps him from hanging. No doubt we will find the Golden Rule somewhat like that. The Golden Rule is spoken by Jesus about God, but the Holy Spirit helps us keep it. The Trinity becomes important in order to have a full capacity to observe the whole rule. The Golden Rule implies that love is both the origin and destination of creation— and that sin is the incapacity or unwillingness to love.

The incarnation of God in flesh, in Jesus, gets very "stubby." It is a short, almost brutal, nonnegotiable fact of our faith. In the Spanish word *encarnacion*, Hispanics see it as making meat of Jesus. Meat lives; meat dies. There is something very fresh and in the minute about meat. It is not universal in a temporal sense. Many people try to make religion bigger and more universal. They do not feel fully spiritual if they are in the daily world of meat. Perspective is often important when the word *love* is being thrown around. Artists know: to make one thing larger in a picture, sometimes other things have to become smaller. To make God first in our life is to get the capacity for love. But first we have to obey the rule and get the size of the picture right.

Theologians like Karl Barth argue that our language about God should begin with language about Christ. For Hispanics, the incarnation exemplifies the ultimate *mestizaje*, the juncture of divinity and humanity, heaven and earth, eternity and real time. Both the Germans and the American Hispanics argue for Christ in a way that the Unitarians do not. Their historical experience made them want a larger, further away God; others wanted a God closer up.

According to Orlando Costas, the incarnation forces us to contextualize God's activity within history, preventing us from turning God into an abstract being removed from human experience. Unfortunately, American Protestants have been more than capable of turning God into a static and abstract notion removed from the immediacy of human experience.[4]

Even when we think we are simple and safe, as in the observance of the Golden Rule, often we are not. Often we are much closer to heaven than we imagine. Jesus lived "off the reservation," often speaking a word others did not want to hear. Some words, especially the first part of the Golden Rule, are too hard to hear. Off the reservation, which is an expression current in military and political circles, designates someone who does not conform to the limits and boundaries of officialdom, who is unpredictable and thus uncontrollable. Native Americans who went off the reservation were summarily shot, for example. A lot of Americans can get by with the bologna cross, looking good by obeying what they think is the Golden Rule. But were it to actually apply to life, a great deal would be significantly different.

Cassie Bernall was a seventeen-year-old junior at Columbine High School. She wore a bracelet that said, "What would Jesus do?" When the kids with the guns came into the library, they asked, "Does anyone here believe in Jesus?" Carrie said yes and was shot to death. Saints often stand up for Jesus. They are often summarily shot, if not with guns, then with the words "loose cannons," "uncontrollable," "not our kind," or "too intense."

Our churches are in one of those denominational periods when we are going to have to decide whether we stand up for Jesus and the ones Jesus loves, the great multitudes of the marginal, including dorks, geeks, murderers, and so-called welfare cheats, or unlucky people who can never pay back their loans. We have been a collective renegade as a nation; as the clouds clear, many of us will be making decisions about whether we want to continue as creative renegades or become a "discount church," searching the web for the safest ride we can get for the cheapest fare. The American church has decisions to make: we need people who will live off the reservation for the reservation—not just off and out and autonomous and opinionated. Not that, not any more. They must live off the reservation for the reservation: fully covenanted, fully autonomous, cloud-clearing saints.

The capacity to love derives from God's love for us. Moral distress, the incapacity to love, is comforted and healed because of God's love. Not ours. Thus, the most off the reservation thing one could do is to really obey the Golden Rule and have God fundamental and first in one's life.

At the end of these three little sessions, we might hope to be even more humble about what we know about God—while knowing much more than we did when we started. Betty Stookey, a local school chaplain, put her faith in this way: "For myself, I believe that the divine mystery I call God is One. That it is the same One that the Muslims call upon, the same One the Christians recognize in Jesus, the same One that the Buddhists seek within, the same One honored by the Jews, the same One seen in nature by the Pagans, and the same One denied by the Atheists."[5] She joins many well-educated Christians in pointing to the God beyond God. Mahatma Gandhi felt similarly: "Religions are different roads converging to the same point. What does it matter that we take different roads, so long as we reach the same goal? In reality, there are as many religions as there are individuals."[6]

Sample Altar Call: Study Scripture

Those who know a little about God want to know more. They are eager to study scripture and to know what the tradition knows about who God is. Daily devotionals abound, and they are a good way to connect to scripture in a vernacular way.

Another good practice is to give ourselves an assignment: for example, "I will read all four Gospels this winter, the Psalms in the summer, the Epistles in the fall, and the five books of the Torah in the spring." That way—or in some other equally structured way—we do not overload ourselves so much as we discipline ourselves to a small portion of the Word of God each season.

Still another method is to pick a daily devotional and memorize its verse. After reading the selection, we can "carry" the verse with us during our day. By the end of a year, we will know several scripture that will come with us as we do our witnessing, our church work, and our daily living.

If none of these methods works for you, if perhaps they are too private, then a Bible study group might be what you need. They abound. Do not be afraid to leave after a session or two if the group is not for you; find one that is right, and stick with it. Both you and God will be pleased.

Chapter 8

The Matter of Mission

◆ ◆

Saved people do something in the world for God. Their knowledge of the Holy moves them to action. They do not just think differently about time or commandments or God's Jubilee promises. They act on behalf of these different thoughts. They live as though God's promises were real; they live outside the world's illusions.

The main obstacle for saved people is the privatized, personal property God. This God has been castrated, made useless, put on a shelf, kept out of the world. This God is not the God of scriptures who acts in history, but the dead God of human fear. Some have spoken of tradition as either the dead faith of the living or the living faith of the dead. I prefer the latter. Traditional interpretations of God always show God alive in history, not dead in history. For example in the Exodus or in the Resurrection, God acts in history on behalf of humanity.

When mission comes alive in people, it is because they remember the action of God in history. They begin to write themselves into God's current action; we write ourselves into the story the way children use life-size manger figures to tell the story of Jesus' birth. We put ourselves in God's story: we act for and with God. That kind of action all but eliminates moral distress in us. We become morally capable because of our partnership with God.

For public ministry to manage and become itself, God must become a subject to us. God is an object in the privatized and disconnected scheme of things. The lack of covenant in our worldview becomes a lack of covenant in our theology. God is a stranger, an other, a "not me," and therefore, we do not have the security of God as fellow traveler, except as we do mental gymnastics that predate the modern period.

Objectification is the intentional move away from relationship with God. God becomes a nonsubject instead of an object. This breaking of covenant, which is the word we often use for God's eternal relationship with humankind and our response to it, makes mission nearly impossible. On our own we will not feed the hungry. With God anything is possible.

The objectification of God hurts real people in real ways. It is the source of the ease of our racism and sexism and is thereby the base of our moral weakness. If it were only morally wrong, that would be one thing, but it is also self-abuse: we hurt ourselves by these objectifications. We isolate ourselves, we lose confidence in ourselves, and we create an unsupporting, ugly world, one that just is not that much fun to live in.

An old man cut off his finger while mowing his lawn. The local hospital—which his father had helped build with his own hands—would not take him because he did not have the proper answers to the insurance questions. This man had voted consistently against more social forms of insurance. He never missed a chance to talk about getting the outsiders and the others out of his community. When he became an other himself, he saw the results of his own isolation. What goes around, comes around. He could not believe that he was no longer an insider in the place where he was born. He could not believe that no one was an insider any more, no one a subject, that we had learned how to treat everyone, even God, as an outsider and an object.

If these privations of privatism were only a problem in the larger community and we could shelter ourselves from them in the church, then it would make sense for churches to build larger fences and keep their doors locked, even more often than they do, but there is no immunity from the objectified community in the church.

Every one of these distancing object makers, from personal through environmental—including theological—and back, seeps into church life. Clergy allowed Clinical Pastoral Education (CPE) to psychologize their vocabulary so they could appear more expert to their membership. Astoundingly, we wanted something that would keep us from identifying so much with our people! We go to workshops learning how to better refer our people to the "appropriate parts" person. Adult Children of Alcoholics? See so and so. Agoraphobic? See such and such. Like the eye doctor who sees only eyes and the ear doctor who sees only ears, we have participated in our own fragmentation. Before you can make a thing a thing, you have to tear it up into little parts. The fragmentation of the experts would be fine if they had left something in the center: they did not. The center is gone.

When clergy were not learning the expertise of psychology, and abandoning their own generalist biblical language in the process, they were learning the expertise of management. The typical pastor is a psychologized manager, or a managerial psychologist: he or she heads a large corporation, the church, and the place is neither mentally healthy or efficiently run. It is not supposed to be either but rather a place of salvation, of humanity being most itself in partnership with God, but that goal has no respect in this age. We respect the time period and become it. If objectification of mowed off fingers is the wisdom of culture, way too many of us are willing to accept it and live by its rules. Culture crucifies Christ, and on the way, many of us know little crucifixions as well.

Can it be any wonder that in the church, with all this loss and the layers of denial that cover the loss, we are constantly berated to uplift, to preach something positive so people can get through their week? No matter: the Bible does not consent to this self-centeredness. It does not offer a cross-less Christianity. It offers one with a cross.

Walter Brueggemann, the preeminent Old Testament scholar of our age, insists that the central theme of that testament is God's action in history to redistribute power. The Jubilee is only one of many ways God keeps breaking back into history to restore original justice. The Jubilee is cross before it is crown.

The lethal weapon we use against God's mission in our age is the refusal to covenant, to stay in relationship with God as subject. Once we return to covenant with the active God, our mission just rolls off the tips of our fingers. Estranged from the active God, enjoying the illusion that God is impotent, we are incapable of mission. Yes, we can do things, but they will have no power.

The professionalization of the vocation of pastor is just one feature of the objectified God. Emily Dickinson said that if we had to see all the truth at once we would all be blind. Maybe that was why we transformed the truth of God into something professional and manageable. Just as lawyers make tracks from justice and teachers distance from learning, pastors remove themselves from pastoring. They try to heal rather than lead, try to fix rather than transform. They put themselves in the place where both God and community belong. They put themselves "above" relationship.

What the church can do to enhance mission is restore our friendship and intimacy with God. The advantages of church ministry for public ministry lie less in its small scale institutional adequacy and more in its biblical capacity to make the right promises and to help people get reacquainted with God as partner and friend.

Our powerlessness to protect the heavens is of one piece. Our God is neither mutual nor dependent, friend nor partner. Our participation in an economy so lethal that it puts holes in the ozone layer is the same. Our public failure is as painful as the private failure to feed our people; each derives from the theological error of not befriending the God who has befriended us.

Youth, like they did in the age of Jonathan Edwards—a prominent, early American preacher—either shun or do not understand the message. They want something different from church, not more management and more therapy. They have enough of that in the world they see every day, a world that rapidly grows in its capacity to use them up.

Edwards's church got into trouble because of its disrespect of youth. When all was said and done, it was because the parents no longer had any land to pass on to their children and that was why they were leaving both the church and the countryside in droves. That was why they disrespected Edwards himself. Edwards sort of understood and tried to explain this to his parishioners in Northampton. They rejected his explanation, just like most parents today would reject the explanation offered here.

Youth are not as dumb as most people like to think they are. They realize that parents have no moral land to pass on. Very few parents have a friendship with God. That lack of friendship shows in the high levels of anxiety and control with which they manage what land they do have. Youth want something different; they want spiritual land. They want to know something of God. Again the economic and spiritual aspects of inheritance are of one piece.

Often churches operate with the hidden curriculum that if you work harder, you will be loved and accepted and everything will be fine for you. Youth know this is no longer true for them in the current economy. That is why they do not listen to clergy: they serve youth stones instead of bread.

If you add the sociological problems of the church to these systemic seepings from the culture and our deeply hidden God, you see that what is advocated here concerning the church as a site of positive public ministry is at best a treasure in a broken vessel. Once we lost our God—or could not see our God anymore—the sociological problems rushed in.

These problems include at least the loss of status of the clergy in the eyes of some older adults. They see the ordination of women and the advent of the two-career family as devastating to the volunteer labor force on which most churches once depended. These perceived institutional weaknesses have become so worrisome to older people that they have trouble finding their God. Clergy are also anxious theologically, so they become more and more interested in therapy and management as ways to stem the tide. Obviously the solution of befriending God would work much better to stem the tide, but clergy would have to fight culture to go in this direction; people would have to have more genuine experience of the Holy than we do.

One image describes the current church most forcefully. In many churches, AA meets downstairs and the congregation meets upstairs. The congregation rarely compares well to the confessed and confessing sinners of AA. At least the members of AA acknowledge their loss and, hard as it is to admit, it brings them more life than the Goody Two-shoes upstairs. God as friend and savior lives downstairs in most churches; upstairs we are still trying to control and manage our loss of the heavens.

The deprivations of privatism are personal and public, economic and sociological, interacting to obscure even God. As AA demonstrates, the possibilities of a more public life are equal in their magnificence to the size of the problem.

Because the church is a David's stone, a mustard seed, a bruised simplicity, its advantages are equal to the obstacles. Facing our loss, stopping the denial of our addiction-like connection to a harmful cultural economy, will lead us to the moment of forgiveness, which is the one that we depend upon to face our loss and go on. Once we have confessed our sins before God, we realize that God has been ready to forgive us for a long time—over and over in fact. Confessing is what the work of cultural remedy will require. We will keep taking that boat back to shore, and God will keep setting us free.

Confession and forgiveness become the remedy for restored mission. These go on to seize a hermeneutical offensive, to comprehend what Thomas Merton described as the hidden wholeness of all things. (Hermeneutical is a big word meaning how we interpret things—whether we let others tell us what is going on or whether we see for ourselves or use God's eyes.) When churches and pastors become capable of seeing how that hidden wholeness and restored sight has a political and public component in our age, we will be restored to the theological work now disguised in work on "the issues." The issue is restoring sight to the blind so that the blind may restore the streets to dwell in.

I repeat Brueggemann's assertion that God's project in history is to redistribute land, to make the valleys plain. Others call repentant justice a level playing field. People in our churches will join God's project as we find God, as we realize how much of God we have actively hidden by cultural commitments.

The gospel is the story of an economic and inner struggle. It connects these struggles rather than fragmenting them. We are each to be involved with both. Public ministry is not making public what was private, rather it is the rejoining of public and private, inner and outer. The restoration of streets to dwell in heals the brokenness of both living rooms and the brokenness of our streets.

This theological initiative is most difficult for First World people, the ones with the choice to return to the shore and live there. We are more able to associate our Christ with our culture than with those who are excluded by it. Alice Walker speaks of our lavender compared to her purple, and I think she has it just right. We can always teach ourselves to prefer the modest and boring security of "white bread,"

American culture to the life of risk described in the gospel. Our loss will be severe, but it will also have a better advertising budget.

Socially and politically the gospel presents itself, these days, in such stark contrast to our culture that it is almost impossible to demonstrate the difference—both impossible and simplistic. The first thing that goes is this fiction of an "I," as though we were "just us." There is no such thing, but most of us live as though there were. Craig Dykstra of the Lilly Endowment writes about church ministry as something that most people think of as something a minister does. That fiction has very little resemblance to the actual web of connections—in, out, up, and down—that a ministry actually is. If you do not believe me, try to do ministry by yourself. You will find how impossible it is.

Once the "I" dissolves as the framework for activity—which is not simple—we have to abandon the language of management and psychology. Then we talk about the church as one of the sites where God and the people are restoring streets to dwell in. The church is not the site where we have our needs met or get things done.

A great game for a gathering is to locate the source of our language at any given moment: rarely will we find that the source is the gospel. We have to learn a new language if the church is to be able to strut its stuff. The language is buried in the gospel.

Another important layer obscuring God, beyond management and psychology, is bureaucracy. John McKnight shows us a picture of genuine community when he inverts the bureaucracy's triangle and organizational chart. In the church, hierarchy usually means the priest and pastor as CEO and the various boards under him or her. Genuine human community inverts that chart and puts the people on the top and the rest as servants to those people. In church life we can experience democracy. We have that choice and that freedom. Adults—not only youth—will like coming to a church that is an alternative to their weekday experience. They will not just like it; they will love it.

The church is also a place where the beatitudes can become true. Where the poor can be experienced as blessing, not burden. There is no need to refer them away especially when we and God need them desperately to make our churches live the gospel.

Obviously this is a tension/conflict model rather than a harmony model. This much institutional change will not be easy. The humor of the conflict is what I call the *peanut butter mentality.* "How," asks one cartoonist, "do you manage a full time job, raising three children and chairing the church bazaar?" She answers her question with, "Oh, it's easy, if you don't mind swimming among alligators who love peanut butter while being covered yourself with peanut butter." The transformation is just that easy: it is a turn in our point of view, fueled by forgiveness, in which we see the difficulties of changes as less than the difficulties of staying the same. Befriended by God, there is little we cannot do or be.

The changed perspective of salvation sees that power, conflict, reconciliation, and redistribution—God's projects in history—have a horizontal and vertical dimension. They are both spiritual matters and economic and political matters. They are each in different stages. There is no separation between my I and our we.

If anything, overly private churches and experiences hurt the individual more than the public ones do. People fear that they will lose their individuality in public actions and relationships when in fact they lose their individuality to mass culture when they refrain from building a healthy, human, friendly culture in which to live. Private needs are better met in more public churches. The Alban Institute has done extensive research on "happy" churches. They distinguish between three types of churches, *a, b,* and *c. Type a* is the happiest and is a church that loves its neighbor as itself. *Type b* is confused and often fights about whether the members are getting enough attention. *Type c* loves its members more than its neighbors and is in steady, serious decline. *Type a* churches grow; the other two types plateau or die and members report serious dissatisfaction in having their personal needs met. As Jesus says, we can have what we can give away. If we cannot give away care, we cannot have it. Those who can love are having more fun than those who are demanding love; the lover has more fun than the beloved—and is more loved!

If the remedy that public ministry offers sounds utopian and evangelical, if it is both-and rather than either-or, if it is to break down the dividing walls of hostility between things earthly of all sorts, it involves a two-step. For the poor it is to assume an epistemological privilege. For the rich it is to let go of a loss-producing epistemological privilege. Public ministry heals us of privatism by ending our blindness to our own loss. It shows us where God has been all the time while we have been wandering. Congregations are tools of public ministry because they are safe enough places to confront our blindness and full of enough community to let us go beyond the loss to fulfill the promise. Once destroyed by churches, streets are now restored in churches. Once obscured by churches, God can also be seen through them now.

Sample Altar Call: Pray

Prayer, for me, is conversation with God. There are moments when I know viscerally that God is near—and plenty of time when I have forgotten. God does not go away at these times; I do.

Just the other day the light green of early spring, the baby budding of trees that I glimpsed through my car window evoked a wowful, thankful moment in me, and God was my partner. Moments later I arrived at my destination to discover a child who had been left alone. As it turned out, she had been left alone for days. No one could have managed my sighs in the moment of first discovery but God. I had gone from praise to lament in miles and minutes. I meant it when I said, "Oh, my God!" I was praying the whole journey through by practicing the presence of God.

We can also pray for ourselves. I ask for discernment in a seemingly endless range of choices: about what to do today or tomorrow, what to say where and when and to whom. Prayer, for me, is focus. It is peeling away the levels and layers of clutter so that I can find out what is truly important at any given time. Praise comes naturally; sighs come frequently. Discernment is what I pray for.

Focus comes to me through God, not through my own powers. On my own, I am a scattered, fragmented do-it-all, know-it-all. Amnesia makes me self-obsessed. Through God, from time to time, I am capable of finding what I must know and finding what I must do. I am also capable of lessening what I missed or forgot.

Again, individual prayer in an individual way may not be the best way for you. You may be the kind of person who will do better with

The Book of Common Prayer, which is an English and Episcopalian daily, weekly, and monthly pattern for praying. Or you may need to simply say the Lord's Prayer every day. The point is less *how* you converse with God and more that you *do* converse with God.

It may take you a little while to develop a personal pattern. Don't fret: Rome was not built in a day. Try several different ways—then make one your habit.

Chapter 9

The Matter of Conversion

◆ ◆

Saved people know how to turn ourselves around. We are turned around by our relationship with the Holy. We become new. Many of us have been rendered silent by our longing for God. We do not experience God so much as we *want* to experience God. We yearn for our God. We long for God. But we do not know God.

I fear the silence is evil, if evil is defined as distance from God. I fear it is active evil, which is to say sin, *incurvatus in se*, according to Luther; missing the mark, according to the Marcan Gospel; or sloth, as the church fathers enumerated one of the seven deadly sins. I fear it is committed sin, not just omitted sin. We "do" the silence in many of my churches. My concern is "small e" evil or lite evil or little evil or trifling banality. According to Hannah Arendt in *The Banality of Evil*, we do not have enough relationship with God to understand how sinful not having one is. We are very far from the Holy.

In the 107 churches that I had ecclesial responsibility for as a supervising pastor, about one-third of them were so alive to the gospel that they give me goosebumps. Jesus lives in them; they are the Body of Christ. Some of them are enormously successful enterprises, with megaprograms, well-painted steeples, and crowds at the door. Others are peeling in more than one way, but they still touch the marginal in their communities in gorgeous ways. Some answer the alarm that all of their communities sound. The alarm: silly schools, globalizing economy, jobs that are boring, HIV/AIDS, Columbine-type kids roaming alone on their streets. However, if they are hanging out in western Massachusetts, they are certainly a minority.

Another third of my "parish," or corner of God's enormous world, was at best in plateau. They were confused. They did not do much besides worry about what they might do or who they might be. Still another third was dead as a doornail, with a few so-called faithful barring the door on anything that might approximate mission or ministry. Christ may live as a still, small voice in some of them, but they make certain that no one knows! They have terminal laryngitis about the wonderful love of their blessed redeemer buried in the depth of their hearts.

Although I wish my district had been exceptional, it fairly represented mainstream Protestantism, a former "city on the hill"—now deeply wounded at being only just another neighborhood, deep in grief over lost triumphalism or imperialism, broken closed not broken open. I want to know how I, as an ordained minister in the church of Jesus Christ, may dare to address this sinful, trivializing silence. In the richest country in the world, in the best-educated denomination, my people—two to one—are boring God stiff. *Metanoia*—the Greek word for conversion meaning "turning, repentant turning"—is the answer. God can forgive what I cannot. God has more mercy than humanity has sin. In some uncanny way, Jesus died for these sins.

Abraham Joshual Heschel said that everyone is responsible even though only some are guilty. We all have an accountability in the matter of the felt absence of the Holy in the mainstream churches. Obviously, God has not gone from us. Instead, we have gone from God. God wants something from me—and you—with regard to the silence and the sin. We were each made in the *Imago Dei*: God did something and made me capable of doing something.

The Three Rs of repentance, resurrection, and reconciliation are all involved in our turning. In repentance we are told to "go and sin no more." In resurrection "the dead have been raised and can be raised again." In reconciliation, the action of bringing things back together is promised. Reconciliation includes judgment and accountability. The only sin God cannot forgive is hardness of heart. Is that what we are looking at? Is our sin terminal despair about the power of God or "functional atheism"?

Issues of retaliation are involved in reconciliation. Unlimited retaliation or limited retaliation: how do Christians get punished? Or punish others—for keeping their light under a bushel or for starving their communities, in the way that Rosemary Ruether calls "Eucharistic starvation."[1] How do I get over my own anger and judgment regarding the lost God of Protestant faith? Obviously, forgiveness and confession come to mind. We develop rituals of reconciliation, repentance, and resurrection. These rituals do not necessarily happen in church or liturgy. Instead, they happen as people get broken open and move out of their state of being closed. Often they happen in meetings.

I am being forced to the nonviolent love of Christ, which is beyond my anger, but my anger is enormous and real. I am in a fairly permanent state of being angry at my own people. My best strategy to move toward these three Rs has been to take middle-class people to the places where people hurt—if they will go, and more than a few will. We plunge them into inner-city areas or tell stories about children. These open people up. When they hear the stories of three thousand street children—better yet children who live on the street—in Capetown, South Africa, they are not as capable of keeping distance from God or these kids. Ironically, these kids carry God to them. When they hear that one in eighteen Capetonians have HIV/AIDS, they do care. Then they go into moral distress or hardness or self-protection. But once people have had one experience of the Holy, they are capable of having more.

Letty Russell, Yale theologian, says ministry is a nonhierarchical partnership. I believe this but often use my judgment to stand above the people. I also use it so I do not have to face the pain of those whom Christ loves especially. I am in need of a personal three Rs—so I can be closer to the love of God, not miss the mark so much, and not be curved in on myself so much. I am constantly reminded of Paul's words that "all have sinned and fall short of the glory of God" (Romans 3:23). We are all part of the distancing.

For me worship is often the best way to break down the hardness I pick up daily in my work. Singing softens me. I can even sing with people I am angry at. For Marva Dawn, an expert on worship, "the community is healthiest when it sings. Singing is the process of creating a communal voice. Singing together expresses the community on a level that goes beyond anything you hear, see, or say." She wants people to feel that "if they don't sing, they are going to die."[2]

Dawn rightly fears that "we have (not been) . . . conducting worship that is deep enough to equip people to lay down the world's follies and shoulder the cross."[3] But those who know the Holy find that God conducts our worship with us. Things happen once we are broken open to the experience of the Holy.

What music cannot heal, prayer can. I often repeat a version of the Shema to recenter myself on God's promises. You may want to memorize Psalm 23 or the Lord's Prayer instead. People who know the Holy pray; prayer is the practice of the presence of God. It is crucial to relationship with God. Even if we are preforgiveness or deep in anger, we can say a prayer of praise to God.

What singing and prayer cannot soften, being among the poor can. For me, as a liberal American, nothing can rival hearing the deep intensity of faith of well-educated world speakers who live in what has been called the Third World. I never miss one when they come to town. Some of these people believe in God in a way that I have not been able to do for years. They really believe that God is going to save the poor. When they speak of Kosovo or East Timor or Chechnya, with accents strange to me, it is with a primary concern, a concern like the one they believe God has for these forlorn places. For me, such matters, if they get on my television screen at all, are secondary or tertiary. Two-thirds of all world speakers see their fate as tied up with the fate of the forlorn. Their educated earnestness accents a different syllable than the cynical; it is, forgive my earnestness, inspirational.

An imam from Istanbul told me at a recent lecture at the World Parliament of Religions in South Africa:

> There is to be no exploitation of anyone, according to Allah. That means if a Christian or a Jew is being exploited, I must stop them. . . . Life is to not only be protected but also promoted. . . . When we have a creative rather than a dogmatic interpretation of religions, a kind of happiness in the individual psyche can happen. . . . We believe that truth is ultimately one. This is different than saying that truth has many faces. . . . We are against the relativism of the postmodernism. . . . They say "do not impose any venue,"

and we know that is a venue itself. . . . Does interreligious dialogue matter to the world at all? Yes, resoundingly.[4]

This same man opened his speech with the word, "Gentlemen" to a mixed crowd of three hundred people. I caught the eye of a woman in a veil right behind me. She lifted her arms as if to say, "Ay, vey." We winked at each other—she from inside, me from outside the veil imposed on us by an otherwise intelligent man. Even inspiration comes in earthen vessels.

This speaker did what any good speaker would do: he commented on the local news broadcast, from what can only be called African Public Radio, or Radio Sonder Grense, FM. This station had been widely discussing the World Parliament, with call-ins every afternoon. Most of those who call in think religion is irrelevant, but a few want to make a point about homosexual unions (these marriages had just been legitimated by the South African government). This speaker called such marriages an abomination. When I objected during the question and answer period, he referred me to scripture and got the resounding approval of the crowd. I made a dozen new friends by saying something, but it was clear that the majority of the crowd did not approve of homosexuality.

When we hear diverse witnesses to God, our hoped for simple conversion becomes difficult. When we have turned toward God, we get to turn again and again. Holiness has never meant moral perfection. Nor has it ever meant permanent simplicity. Holy Ones are appealing and attractive; they shape a witness to the flourishing that God wills for all of earth's creatures. They show us the church of the "here and there, now and then" in William Stringfellow's apt words.[5] The experience of the Holy puts us in the mood for the hymn "Holy, Holy, Holy" and its profound assertion that *only thou art holy*. It does not remove us from complexity. Instead we get what Evelyn Underhill calls a joy that cannot be altered by any circumstance.

If songs or prayer or good speeches do not bring you remembrance of the Holy in your life, you may want to develop a customized daily discipline. One friend of mine insists that he places himself in the way of beauty every day. Another simply sits. We have to beware of a vicarious holiness, where we pretend that something is going on that is not. God is not mocked. Holiness is genuine intimacy with God, intimacy in which "nearer my God to thee" is an actual plea or a time when all you can do is kneel.

I am always fascinated by youthful slang. Two favorite words are: *awesome* and *duh*—the latter meaning, "How obvious. Don't you get it?" This slang could be used to attend to the Holy, that which demands our complete attention. When the veil on God is lifted, things get a little spooky. We are changed. We are converted. We have new sources of energy.

Mary Luti, a theologian from Andover Newton and a former nun, says these are the categories of classical holiness:

- **Martyrdom:** when we are willing to die for our God and do so gladly.

- **Asceticism:** when we purposefully make ourselves strangers to the world. The ascetics became such strangers to the world that death has little to take from them. Thus they were trusted. They had no vested interest in the world.

- **Zeal:** when we are capable of the great deeds of the miracle worker, like a Carnegie.

- **Stigmata:** when we announce what we have done for God.

- **Sanctification:** where we are known by others to have been sanctified.[11]

In *Embodied Holiness: Toward a Corporate Theology of Spiritual Growth*, Stanley Hauerwas, a Duke University theologian and ethicist, tells us holiness has not so much to do with our souls as with our bodies. Hauerwas argues that no Christian ethic is worthwhile unless it can be understood and practiced by a medieval peasant; then he mischievously suggests that modern-day professionals are actually more like peasants than they realize. As for peasants, and for us, Hauerwas suggests: the body, with its diseases and its habits, is the place where we find sanctification. This very provocative thought, based in the Wesleyan tradition of a demonstrated holiness, connects quite well to the classical signs; it tells us why cancer is often such a moving experience for people—one that moves them right to God. Muriel Rukeyser says that we should breathe experience in, breathe out poetry. Even the ancients knew there was no one way to experience the holy; we have to make our own poetry of it. Some of the poetry will last and last and others will be like the air that blows beautifully away. We will want "wood that will not rot," as in the promise of Isaiah 40:20, but we will not be able to control what our God gives us. That is the point of holiness: we realize we are not in charge and God is.

Dan Sullivan, in *How the Best Got Better*, advises business managers to "break through the ceiling of complexity" and "move to a new state of simplicity."[7] Not one of the solutions is to trick the manager, as the dishonest manager does in Luke 16, paying back fifty jugs for one hundred jugs of oil or returning eighty containers of wheat for the one hundred borrowed. The dishonest manager tries to trick God, tries to control God, tries to set things up his way rather than God's way. Once we have known conversion, we are not immune from more sin.

Instead of being dishonest stewards, Sullivan advises that people "depend entirely on their own abilities . . . and create something good for another person."[8] Instead of giving back less, we are to give out more. This management advice echoes the Golden Rule and many of Jesus' sayings: if someone wants your scarf, give them your coat also. Do unto others what you want done to you. Give what you want; you will get it that way in return.

Most of us would love a gift. Almost any gift. We may experience the presence of God as a gift and still experience our church as stingy. We can change these churches—even, and especially as we have been changed. Instead of a deacon asking for more from the pastor, the deacon might release the pastor from something: "I'll visit the nursing home next week." Instead of the pastor asking for more from the deacons, the pastor might suggest a shorter meeting some night. Instead of missing the secretary's bulletin deadline (again), we could work a week or two ahead of schedule. We can create value in simple ways. We can untie the knots. We can get out of the traffic jam that often occurs in busy, if not converted, churches.

These "little" moves are not done alone. They are done to nudge the system into its own health. Sullivan advises never using the words, "I can do it by myself."[9] We make a personal paradigm shift every time we prod the system into greater webbed value.

Sullivan speaks of "past based selves" who still fantasize that someone above them has responsibility for their life and "future based selves"[10] who know they are on their own, with God, in a gift-giving context. Instead of being trapped by their weaknesses, future-based individuals are free to focus entirely on their strengths. A past-based self resists anything new. A future-based self responds to new and bigger challenges. After people begin to depend entirely on their own abilities for economic security, the second decision is to expect opportunity in life by first creating value for others. Future-based selves say good-bye to entitlement. The experience of holiness is not an experience of entitlement: rather its conversion turns us more towards our own capacity to give.

We change our days, our *lo quotidiano*, as much as we change our attitudes toward our days, our time, and our relationships. For example, Sullivan advocates three kinds of days to replace the clocked eight-hour day: *buffer days, free days,* and *focus days.* He advocates "the no office solution," arguing that bureaucracy derives from the "rule of the desk or office."[11] Therefore, organizations (maybe churches) should get rid of the office and create a superb meeting room. Radical idea, right?

The key question honest managers ask is, "If we were meeting three years from today, what has to have happened during that three year period for you to feel happy about your progress?" Sullivan advises that we can escape from the crisis of the dishonest manager—the complexity of too much happening, not enough time to think and learn, too little security, not enough opportunity, too few resources, not enough leverage—into economic adulthood. I not only believe he is right, I believe this is exactly what Jesus promised to the dishonest steward: a way to honor God in the way we work. Nothing more. And nothing less.

Another way to speak of holiness is to say that once we know God we become spiritually gifted people. Spiritually gifted people are intimate with God. They may memorize a verse or two of the Bible every day, but they do not call it memorization; they never eat without thanking God; they are often the spiritual engine of their church; they pray regularly; they know the sheer power of Spirit; they may cloister from time to time; they tithe; they witness; they are part of a group who knows them through and through and still loves them all in all; they have extraordinary hope for and in the poor. Are you one of them? Who in your congregation is? Pray for them. Pray to become one.

Holiness changes people. God changes people into poets, Holy ones, free ones, people who are *altared* and who respond to the call.

Sample Altar Call: Act for Mission

An intentional, daily or weekly practice of doing something for somebody besides yourself will take your response to the gospel a long way. In Numbers 15:37-38 we are told to "put a blue cord on the fringe at each corner. You have the fringe so that, when you see it, you will remember." Mission is the active act of remembrance that we live in God's time, not in human time. God is making the world new. God's purpose in history is to make the world new. There is no doubt that the time of God's justice—the kingdom, the commonwealth—is on its way. We "fringe" ourselves by being part of the new time in a disciplined way.

Doing mission may mean writing a letter to your congressman or mayor, visiting the local juvenile court and adopting one youth offender, being a Big Brother or Sister, behaving ethically in the work place, or acting for justice for a fellow employee. It may mean being an active part of a mission committee or task group. It connects to tithe and witness and prayer—but it also transcends them. When we fringe ourselves with mission, we act with God in God's time for justice.

Chapter 10

The Call to Hospitality

◆ ◆

W hen we know that we are saved, when we are practicing the presence of God through our use of time and money, when we are part of a group that knows us through and through and loves us the same way, when we are part of a church structured for mission, we find ourselves uncannily hospitable. We are genuinely open to the other as a friend. We borrow some of God's love; we make space for the stranger.

When we keep Sabbath and find a regular way to rest, pray, study, live, we are able to be genuinely open to other people. Hospitality is the experience of the other as our own; it is the opposite of hostility, which turns the other into a *hostes*, or enemy.

The last way we respond to our salvation is in the experience of ourselves as genuinely, strategically, and institutionally hospitable. Those of us in mainstream churches have a real struggle here: we have been labeled as inhospitable. Even *Saturday Night Live*, the television show, parodies the church lady as cramped and tight and mean. We have a large stereotype to overcome.

Why should anyone care whether denominations or institutions are perceived as inhospitable? What are the stakes of weakened institutions for spiritual life? Aren't they obstacles anyway? A singles ministry in Worcester, Massachusetts, attracts three hundred people on Friday night for prayer and song. How? By rigorously assuring that they have no denominational label. The Vineyard Movement, rapidly developing into a paradenominational structure, sustains the largest membership growth of any contemporary religious movement by vigorously defining itself outside organized religious structures.

Denomination is neutral enough as a word. It means: the act of naming or a name—more specifically, the name of a class of things.

Denomination comes from the Latin designation that means to name out a class or a kind, having a specific name or value, as in coins of a different denomination. We would not have denominations if we had not had the Reformation. We would have only had one holy Catholic Church. Ironically, in an age of increasing tolerance of religious diversity, denominations have developed a bad name. The religious impulse toward unity—or the widely felt belief that "there is only one God"—undercuts the division into denominations of the Christian faith.

Both the word *denomination* and its companion *denominator* have moved beyond a neutral connotation in their most common expressions. We almost always hear denominator in partnership with "the lowest common" as in the "lowest common denominator." Oddly, this derogatory sense that blending is bad wars with the departure by many people from the particularity of diverse classes of religion. If blend is bad, why isn't distinction good? Mainstream churches find themselves, as a result of this struggle, in a situation where hospitality is hard for us to offer. We may feel hospitable as a church or as a person—but others see us and assume we are not.

Mainstream denominations have a fence to jump in order to be genuinely hospitable. There are spiritual changes and practical changes we can make. Both are needed. The spiritual change is again confessional: perhaps we are genuinely inhospitable. Perhaps we are as afraid of the other as we are welcoming of him or her. If that is the case, it is best that we admit it early and often, rather than deny it.

Any church that wants to move into active experience of its salvation will not be afraid of the harshness of such a question. It will understand that God can forgive even the most base of hypocrisies and inhospitalities. God understands our fears. It is not unreasonable to be afraid of the other or to see the other as a stranger or a threat. It is actually quite reasonable! But that fear changes to love when we ourselves are secure in our salvation. Mainstream denominations do not need to wag their fingers at themselves so much as they need to embrace the genuine love of God. God's hospitality to us makes our hospitality to others possible.

The list of incongruities only begins with understanding the underground life of "very friendly" churches. There are also barriers to hospitality in other myths of the modern period. We are almost afraid to be ourselves! "Just Methodists" or "just Presbyterians" is a phrase one hears quite often. We know we are not enough just the way we are—but we also know, simultaneously, that the experience of grace is precisely to be enough as we are. "Just as I am, without one plea," we sing.

We have an increasing distaste for the particular in religion, especially when it takes on universal attributes, at the same time that we have an increasing distaste for the cookie cutter nature of the general. We like neither the particular nor the general very much. This irony puts denominations in a lose/lose situation. The more particularly they define their identities, the more likely they are to invoke the word "better" when it comes to themselves; they are less likely to declare universality because religious tolerance has become king on the religious value scale. Simultaneously, the more they invoke the general, the more likely they are to be diluted versions of faith. One friend swears her local Presbyterian church is the General Foods and General Motors of its genre. The Church of All Things to All People is what she calls it.

Having gone from writing "none" in the religious box on college applications to exploding the line with blends and hyphenations, Americans are rapidly moving beyond the particularity of their heritage. It is nothing to meet a former Lutheran who is now Buddhist, belongs to a Methodist church, and worships there regularly. People have blended and moved way beyond the denominations of their origins. We want a place to befriend us more than ever before, but numerous barriers litter our way. In a world where people may easily work in two or three time zones a day, speak several languages, and travel the Internet to an on-line Chinese conference, the notion of God as being Methodist or Presbyterian is absurd. God clearly does not speak just English, and he is not just Episcopalian.

One of the stakes in the demise of denominations as a significant religious vessel is the truth about God and about faith. If God has broken the denominational boundaries and geographical boundaries, how dare we keep God captive. The stakes in "open" and "tolerant" denominational structures are extraordinarily large. Keeping the open denomination friendly is a matter of no small consequence.

113

The Dalai Lama, who has attracted many foreigners as followers, tells people not to become Buddhist but to go home and become what they are supposed to become. He can get away with it with Americans because he is an "exotic." Postdenominational American Christians are increasingly having a hard time naming the name of Christ. The reason is they are caught between their own inherited particularity and the fear that they will tyrannize in the name of Christ. Nevertheless, many will argue that the very demise of denominations is related to this lack of an ability to name the Christ unimperially. Truly hospitable people are so comfortable with their own salvation that they do not force it on others. Their salvation is a wood that does not rot. As stated in Isaiah 40:20: "As a gift one chooses mulberry wood—wood that will not rot—then seeks out a skilled artisan to set up an image that will not topple." Skilled artisans at hospitality know Christ centrally and confidently, but they do not force that gift on others—they show it to others.

One of the best-kept secrets of American life is that those who invest in supportive relationships tend to be the happiest, healthiest, and most productive persons. They have a greater array of resources to face crisis with, and they are likely to recover more quickly following personal and societal tragedy than those who "go it alone." If supportive networks are so important to our well-being, it is vital to understand the character of support. Support is commonly understood to mean "wind at our back," the experience of being held. People who know Jesus as Christ are held; they are therefore able to hold others the way they are held, which is softly and carefully.

I would like a little kindness. The best way for me to get it is to give it. I would like a little empathy. Again, I can have what I can give away. Hospitable people give away what they want to receive, and in that action, they receive it.

Most of us would love a gift—almost any gift. Instead of church leaders asking for more from the pastor, the deacon might release the pastor from something. "I'll visit the nursing home next week." Instead of the pastor asking for more from church leaders, the pastor might suggest a shorter meeting some night, "just for fun." Instead of being late for the secretary's bulletin deadline (again), we might work ahead a week or two. We can create value in simple ways. We can untie the knots. We can get out of the traffic jam that is often in churches. These "little" moves are not done alone. They are done to nudge the system into its own health and its own hospitality. Many of our churches have a ways to go to become healthy enough to be hospitable. Health precedes hospitality in the same way that salvation precedes hospitality. In *Creating a Healthier Church: Family Systems, Leadership, and Congregational Life* by Ronald Richardson, we hear a step-by-step description of how to get healthy after being wounded. In a practical, simplified way, Richardson says the task of ministry is not to be Friedman's nonanxious presence. During the 1990s, Friedman was the guru for "family systems" in congregations; his wisdom had the slogan for ministry being a nonanxious presence or connection. Instead Richardson argues that we should be a *less* anxious presence. He argues that we should become blended and more distinguished, rather than the grandiosity of undifferentiation and complete defusion in our family systems. He moves us beyond fault with a gracious invitation to system-wide health. Basing the entire text on one problem that occurs in two different churches, one unhealthy, the other healthy as a system, he manages to demonstrate different responses to similar difficulties.

Hospitable churches and hospitable people have genuine faith. We also have the capacity for genuine doubt. We are "real" in a way that people can sense. Remember the conversation between the father and his son: "Do you really believe this thing can fly and hold you up?" "I'll tell you the truth, Son, I never did put all my weight down on that plane." Certainty is not hospitable; it is actually quite a scary thing. Something flexible like a doubting faith or a faithful doubt is much more hospitable to the stranger.

Let's go back to the image of the wounded door. That wounded door is the religious authority of me confronting the other and myself, simultaneously. At that nexus or node, I experience Jesus and who and the way he was. From this confrontation—of the outsider in us and the insider in us and how most other people have the same "insides"—we develop very practical baby steps to freely connect people to each other and to congregations and denominations.

We train greeters; we wear nametags; we do not make "in-house" announcements that newcomers cannot understand. We become transparent as an organization *because we want to be hospitable to the outsider*. Deep reasons undergird practical matters.

A simple experience may help. One day I was on the podium of an extraordinarily tedious, yet joyful, church service in which the local clergy had been gathered by the local African American church to give God orders on the abolishment of racism. We called these orders "prayers." Another policeman had shot another black teenager "by accident." We had to gather. We had to pray. We could not help ourselves from turning our prayers into orders. We did not trust God so much as we needed God. Our need snuck into our language. One after another of us prayed. Then we sang. Then we prayed some more. I had a feeling that most of the five hundred people in the congregation were still with us. All of a sudden I got this great urge to leave. Just leave. I had already given God my orders, done my part, lamented my lament. I was no longer needed except as another pair of ears. My chair on the podium was in the back row. I might not be noticed. So I left. I walked out the side door behind the organ and behind the altar. It was dusk. What the poet John Keats called the luxury of twilight enveloped me: I was part of purple air. Even better, I was part of clear air as opposed to the dank air of scared prayer. I was wearing my black liturgical robe, which seemed appropriate to the occasion. I unbuttoned the black robe once I got outside. No one was there but me. The parking lot was full, the church was rocking to another hymn, but I was free. I was alone. I was out. I ran to my car with the robe waving beyond me, and I had the feeling that I might have just escaped God. I might be free of God. I might be free.

These are the only few minutes in my life that I might have been free of God. Otherwise God has been a constant companion, nudge, heartbeat, inner voice, best friend. The strangeness of my little escape startled me. In the startle and the twilight, I realized how I feel about church as religious authority. Church has not always contained God for me. More often, God has been in the streets or the garden or literature. God has been in laughter and in liberation, like skipping the meeting that was pompously discussing God. But God has never been "not there."

That night in the parking lot I experienced the God who was not there as freeing, liberating—only to learn later that it was the church that was driving me crazy. Like the authority of the temple, the church's authority had begun to shrink God. I had no doubt that God had become free, had squeezed out, but I had real doubts about whether I could know God within religious structure alone. That night, God came in the luxury of the twilight. In the racing robe. In the absence of God.

New revelations are needed. I have no problem looking for them in the parking lot. Or in the eyes of my puzzled Jewish husband. I have this urge to look "elsewhere" for God rather than by rounding up the usual suspects. That urge is an urge for authority. It is something that feels deeper than even magnificent African American worship or great table prayers, each of which are sites where I can usually count on God. When I rush to the openings, I am looking not just for God but for more God, for deeper God, for eternal God.

I know God because I am an escape artist. I work the raw openings. Most people find this kind of flexibility infuriating. For me, it gives permission to skip out of services. My faith is in the hallway as much as the sanctuary.

When I speak of hospitality, I know it means the ability to leave as well as the ability to stay. A genuine home sets us free. A genuine welcome is one we do not have to accept. Getting the ought out of church hospitality will go a long way toward letting people be free to be a part of church life. We are called, freely, to the altar. There we may say yes or no. That is the power of the hospitality of God.

Sample Altar Call: Become Deeply Hospitable

Those of us who know the call of the gospel open ourselves to the other—the other within and the other without. Those of us who have been touched by God are open to the stranger. We know the stranger is an angel sent by God to show us something. We have room for what the stranger has to say.

Christians often live off the reservation. We not only befriend mavericks, renegades, and loose cannons; we are often called these "otherizing" names. We are people who go off the reservation on behalf of the reservation. We are not so much anarchists as we are community builders. Our communities are places where strangers are welcome.

The gospel will take us to places of great adventure. It will get us out of "gated" communities or niched places, places where everybody and everything is the same. When we get "outside," we will find ourselves identifying with the others out there. We may even be surprised to find out how many of the ordinary looking members of our ordinary church also feel a little like outsiders themselves!

The gospel opens us up to be genuinely hospitable to outsiders and insiders—and to each of those parts in ourselves.

Notes

◆ ◆

Introduction

1. Ben Watts, class lecture, Hartford Seminary, Spring 1996.
2. Ibid.

1. Salvation as a Response to the Holy

1. Ada Maria Isasi-Diaz, lecture, Union Seminary, November 1998.
2. Daniel F. Chambliss, *Beyond Caring: Hospitals, Nurses, and the Social Organization of Ethics* (Chicago: University of Chicago Press, 1996).
3. Lawrence Friedman, *The Horizontal Society* (New Haven: Yale University Press, 1999).
4. Ibid.

2. Money as a Call from and to the Altar

1. Juliet Schor, *The Overspent American: When Buying Becomes You* (New York: Basic Books, 1998).

3. Sharing Faith in a World of Holy Discontents

1. John Updike, "The Future of Faith: How Long Will It Hold On?" *New Yorker* (November 29, 1999): 91.
2. Lesslie Newbigin, *Foolishness to the Greeks: The Gospel and Western Culture* (Grand Rapids, Mich.: Eerdmans, 1986), 15.
3. Nelson Mandela, lecture, December 1999, World Parliament of Religions in South Africa.
4. Elizabeth Domingues, speech, 1991, United Church of Christ Faith Works Conference.
5. Marva Dawn, *Reaching Out Without Dumbing Down: A Theology of Worship for the Turn-of-the-Century Church* (Grand Rapids, Mich.: Eerdmans, 1995).

119

5. The Matter of the Meeting

1. Charles Olsen, *Transforming Church Boards into Communities of Spiritual Leaders* (Bethesda: Alban Institute, 1995), Appendix 3.

7. The Confidence of Knowing the Basics of Our Faith

1. Kathleen Norris, *Amazing Grace: The Vocabulary of Faith* (New York: Riverhead Books, 1998).
2. Ibid.
3. Ibid.
4. See: Luis Pedraja "Doing Christology in Spanish," *Theology Today* (January 1998).
5. Betty Stookey, Northfield Mt. Hermon, student brochure, 1999.
6. Mahatma Gandhi, sermon, quoted in the Northfield Mt. Hermon student brochure, 1999.

9. The Matter of Conversion

1. Rosemary Ruether, speech, Campus Ministry Women, Cleveland, 1979.
2. Marva Dawn, *A Royal Waste of Time: The Splendor of Worshiping God and Being Church for the World* (Grand Rapids, Mich.: Eerdmans, 1999), 7.
3. Ibid., 8.
4. Member of the Moslem Panel, lecture, January 1999, World Parliament of Religions in South Africa, Capetown.
5. William Stringfellow, sermon, Cleveland, February 1989.
6. Mary Luti, lecture to the Massachusetts Conference Staff, Spring 1998.
7. Dan Sullivan, "How the Best Got Better," business brochure.
8. Ibid., 2.
9. Ibid.
10. Ibid., 3.
11. Ibid.

Resources and References

◆◆

The resource and reference section lists several books that offer methods that can be used to love the world that God has made. Love is what we need. When love is in our response to the holy, when we care about the genuine other out there as much as we care about those inside the church walls, then the methods will come.

Books

An 8-Track Church in a CD World, Robert N. Nash, Jr. (Smyth and Helwys Publishing, 1997). Nash believes that mainline churches, as we have known them, are finished. They no longer bring people to God. They are modern in a postmodern world. They are stuck to the old ways in a world that has moved and changed. People under fifty just do not understand the way older people worship. They need worship that is more like Wal-Mart—lots of options, quick access, nothing regular, not a lot of investment, and great printing. When Nash talks about how church posters are apt to be hand-lettered—and how this makes people think the experience is going to have the same flavor—many of us who still love the old church say, "Ouch." We know what he means. Our methods can make it look like we are not loving.

Amazing Grace: A Vocabulary of Faith, Kathleen Norris (Riverhead Books, 1998).

Awareness, Miriam Adahan (Feldheim, 1994). The first text written on the Enneagram from a Jewish perspective. The Enneagram is a Sufi model of personalities similar to the Meyers Briggs scale.

Beyond Establishment: Protestant Establishment in a Post-Protestant Age, edited by Jackson Carroll and Wade C. Roof (Westminster John Knox, 1993).

Building an Effective Congregational Council, Susan Carloss (Augsburg Fortress, 1992).

Building Effective Boards for Religious Organizations: A Handbook for Trustees, Presidents, and Church Leaders, edited by Thomas P. Holland and David C. Hester (Jossey Bass, 1999). This book summarizes a large amount of contemporary research and is particularly helpful for members of congregations and religious nonprofit organizations that are in the middle of "strategic planning," "visioning," or "long-term planning." The book includes ten essays: four on faithful governance and six on improving the organization's performance—a welcome combination in a world where the myth is that you cannot have both faith and performance. The essays are written by noted individuals who rely on boards to direct their work.

The book ends with an interesting notion that religious institutions are at a turning point, language reminiscent of Victor Turner's liminality or early Dawn. This millennium-friendly notion gives organizations the permission and lightness needed to turn and not be embarrassed at how much turning they seem to need to do.

"Can the Mainline Church Survive?" Don Miller. In *Reinventing American Protestantism: Christianity in the New Millennium* (University of California Press, 1999), pp. 177-90.

Celebrating Our Differences: Living Two Faiths in One Marriage, Mary Helene Rosenbaum and Stanley Ned Rosenbaum (White Mane, 1999). This book is written by a Catholic wife and her Jewish husband, who evolved into his observant Judaism as an adult. It is great, especially if both partners are on the more devout side of practicing their respective faiths. It provides wonderful practical examples on how to weave both traditions into one household.

Christian Basics: A Primer for Pilgrims, Gabriel Fackre and Dorothy Fackre (Eerdmans, 1991) is a narrative and more up to date version of Gabriel Fackre's *The Christian Story: A Narrative Interpretation of Basic Christian Doctrine* (Eerdmans, 1978), which covers God, Creation, the Fall, covenant, Jesus Christ (person and work), the church (its nature and mission), salvation, and consummation. Both of these books cover the same topics in relevant ways. Each de-emphasizes the Holy Spirit, confirming Mary Luti's comment that Protestantism is third-person deficient in its theology. Again, for those who need a very basic place to start, criticism of what we do not have is important to hear. We may not have enough "Spirit" theology, but many people need to walk through what we do have first.

Church for The Unchurched, George G. Hunter, III (Abingdon Press, 1996). Hunter's book makes an uncanny observation: many people do not join churches because "they don't want to become like church people" (p. 59). Those of us raised in the church feel offended at this point—as well as called out of some of our behavior and into new and more genuine ways of representing the gospel. Unfortunately, too many church people are not saturated with the real gospel at all. We are more worried about *gaining* new members than we are about *loving* new members.

Congregations, Stories, and Structures, James Hopewell (Augsburg Fortress Press, 1987).

Constructing Local Theologies, Robert J. Schreiter (Orbis Books, 1993).

Creating a Healthier Church: Family Systems Theory, Leadership, and Congregational Life, Ronald Richardson (Augsburg Fortress, 1996). This book talks about our own anxiety levels, on a scale of 1-100, and the anxiety level of our church systems, on a similar scale. We are helped by excellent questions at the end of each chapter to see how we might reduce the scale of anxiety and promote both our personal and our church's health.

Discovering the Enneagram: An Ancient Tool a New Spiritual Journey, Richard Rohr and Andreas Ebert (Crossroads, 1992).

The Enneagram and the Kabbalah: Reading Your Soul, Howard A. Addison (Jewish Lights, 1998). This work examines what the Enneagram's nine-pointed star and the Sefirot of Kabbalah's Tree of Life have in common. The Enneagram comes from ancient Sufi tradition and the Sefirot is from ancient Jewish tradition. What is astonishing is how similar these personality types—the tree of life and the nine-pointed star—are.

Each of these has a theory of polarity, showing that in great virtue there is great vice and proving that we can only view what we can see from where we are sitting. We cannot see beyond that. If the Meyers Briggs scale of personalities—either intuitive or rational, perceptive or judging—has been an aid to you in your home or office, get this mystical psychology. It will show you why Venus is often so far away from Mars and why there are some people you just do not understand.

Evangelism That Works: How to Reach Changing Generations with the Unchanging Gospel, George Barna, edited by Virginia Woodard (Gospel Light, 1995). In this work, we are called to the authenticity of a befriending God. Barna takes on false culural claims and argues that American culture is more concerned about what people *think* about God than about God (p. 330). What matters to

Barna is that members and pastors have a deep sense of God. The rest will come. Barna gives an excellent list of the thirteen obstacles to evangelism (p. 128). These include, among other things, the absence of prayer, not owning outreach, failure at building bridges, being afraid to seek the right outcome, and decisions—not conversions—for Christ that are getting in people's way. We get stuck outside the gate to God, and too much evangelism gets stuck out there too.

Faith and Fratricide: The Theological Roots of Anti-Semitism, Rosemary Ruether (Wipf and Stock, 1996).

The Gift of Hospitality: In Church, in the Home, in All of Life, Delia Halverson (Chalice Press, 1999). "True hospitality comes from the heart, without any expectation of anything in return" (p. 11). This definition of hospitality pervades the book, releasing it from finger-wagging, church-growth captor into a manual for being church. New members may result from following the instruction provided in this book, but they are not the goal that Halverson is after. She is after genuine hospitality because it is what Jesus would do. This book would make a great short study course in any church—particularly one that feels stuck on the new member issue.

The Intermarriage Handbook: A Guide for Jews and Christians, Judy Petsonk and Jim Remsen (Morrow, 1991). A handbook with lots of practical tips, recommendations, and knowledgeable information. It has quite an insightful chapter on the history of Jews and Christians, which will help any Christian understand the more tribal nature of Judaism. It has a slight bias toward Judaism.

The Jesus Factor: Radical Transformation in Early Christianity, Harry Taylor (published by Christians for Justice Action [CJA], which is a United Church of Christ caucus), discusses controversial issues like homosexuality, women's ordination, and abortion. It is an unpublished look at how both the First and Second Testament viewed these subjects. It is available through the CJA and can be ordered by calling (636)447-6747.

Life Together, Dietrich Bonhoeffer (Harper, 1976).

Living in the Presence: Spiritual Exercises to Open Our Lives to the Awareness of God, Tilden H. Edwards (Harper, 1995).

Making Interfaith Marriage Work: A Nonjudgmental Guide to Coping with the Spiritual, Emotional, and Psychological Issues Facing Every Couple,

Stephen Carr Reuben (Prima Publishing, 1994). A rabbi of a Reconstructionist congregation in Southern California wrote this book, and it is based on years of experience counseling interfaith couples. By nature it is slightly biased toward Judaism, but it contains lots of insight and words of wisdom.

Mere Christianity, C. S. Lewis (Simon & Schuster, 1986), is another good source for someone just beginning to study Christianity. Lewis wrote twenty-three books on the matter of Christianity, including The new *C. S. Lewis Collection* (Harper, 1993)—which is both humorous and critical. He is one of the most accessible authors for the skeptical novice.

Mixed Matches: How to Create Successful Interracial, Interethnic, and Interfaith Marriages, Joel Crohn (Fawcett Columbine/Ballantine Books, 1995). A must-read if a couple is dealing with strong ethnic differences on top of the interfaith issue. Otherwise, the read might be a little academic at times. It also might be a bit broad for those who want to read only about interfaith marriage.

The New Practical Guide for Parish Councils, William Rademacher with Marliss Rogers (Twenty-Third, 1988).

"The Place of the Congregation in the Contemporary American Religious Configuration," Stephen Warner. In *American Congregations: New Perspectives in the Study of Congregations,* (University of Chicago Press, 1994), pp. 54-99.

"Presbyterian Culture: Views from the Edge," Louis B. Weeks. In *Beyond Establishment* (Westminster John Knox, 1993), pp. 309-26.

The Purpose-Driven Church: Growth Without Compromising Your Message and Mission, Rick Warren (Zondervan, 1995). Warren shows how every church is driven by something. If it is healthy, it will grow. The issue is health, not growth. "If your church is healthy, growth will occur naturally. Healthy, consistent growth is the result of balancing the five biblical purposes of the church" (p. 39). Warren also emphasizes good techniques for getting people in the door. Good space, refreshments, a visitor's book, rest rooms, the protection of anonymity, good parking, and the like are given a definite respect. Rather than being strangers to the distribution of the gospel, these matters are considered friends. We are not without method to our foolishness about the completeness of the love of God. Instead, we us methods; they do not use us.

Raising Your Jewish-Christian Child: How Interfaith Parents Can Give Children the Best of Both Heritages, Lee F. Gruzen (Random, 1991). Definitely read this book if the plan is to raise children in both religions. A very hopeful, intelligently written book that validates the "dual-faith upbringing" when so many others do not. The author gives practical examples of how she organized community and children's religious education with other families in the same situation.

Re-Imagining Denominationalism, edited by R. Bruce Mullin and Russell E. Richey (Oxford University Press, 1994).

The Restructuring of American Religion: Society and Faith Since World War II, Robert Wuthnow, edited by John F. Wilson (Princeton University Press, 1988).

Sacred Cows Make Gourmet Burgers: Ministry Anytime Anywhere by Anyone, William M. Easum (Abingdon Press, 1995). In this book, there is a strong critique of mainline churches. This book "outs" a major confusion—which is that people think running churches is ministry, which it is not. It shows us why so many people get hives when asked to serve (I use "serve" advisedly) on a church committee. And it shows how the new age, or quantum age, has no need for the controllers. Radical in its polity, it will surely appeal to the hundreds and thousands of people who would like to be part of the Body of Christ but not the committee of Christ. A permission-giving organization as opposed to a bureaucratic or controlling operation is the antidote to the deviltry of control (p. 97). In permission-giving organizations, anybody—anytime, anywhere—can do ministry.

The theological basis for Easum's near anarchy is that of the church as the Body of Christ. As body parts, feet do not need to ask hands for permission; they need to do their thing and do it well. Easum sees spiritual gifts as feet: they are different but connected to the other parts. They do not need permission from the arms to move; they already have it and should use it.

The Spirit of Protestantism, Robert M. Brown (Oxford University Press, 1965), says, "Protestantism is not 'there,' it is all over the place. It does not have recognizable boundaries; it is extremely difficult to know when an individual or a church has ceased to become Protestant" (p. 206).

One of the things Protestants need to do is create a comfort zone for and around our religious openness. We are intentionally theologically "fluid" already. We want to be a little blurry; we choose to be blurry. When people are more comfortable with this diffuse identity, many will become more certain that they know what it means to be "religious" in a Protestant way.

Spiritual Literacy: Reading the Sacred in Everyday Life, Frederic Brussat and Mary Ann Brussat (Scribner's, 1996), is a good source for the prematurely ecumenical and people who distrust any one religious point of view. It is an encyclopedic volume of spiritual nuggets on subjects like relationships, creativity, and nature. It deftly makes the distinction between the religion of the sanctuary and the spirit of most of our daily lives.

Strangers to the Tribe: Portraits of Interfaith Marriage, Gabrielle Glaser (Houghton Mifflin, 1997). This book contains a series of descriptive chapters, each about an interfaith couple converted to Judaism. The book is also about "strangers" to Judaism. This is a great read for anyone in an interfaith marriage considering conversion to Judaism or maintaining a Jewish household. It is not a how-to by any means, but it is easy to read as one gets absorbed into the different lives of the author's interviewees.

Studying Congregations: A New Handbook, edited by Nancy Ammerman, et al. (Abingdon Press, 1998).

Take and Read: Spiritual Reading: An Annotated List, Eugene H. Peterson (Eerdmans, 1996) gives the interested novice a summary of great Christian devotional material. This book includes devotionals covering Psalms, prayers, worship and liturgy, spiritual formation, pastors, Jesus, history, and several other topics. It also includes some of Peterson's own work, modestly placed at the end of the book.

"Timeless Priorities in Changing Contexts: African Americans and Denominationalism," Lawrence Jones. In *Beyond Establishment,* pp. 228-47.

To Begin at the Beginning: An Introduction to Christian Faith, Martin Copenhaver (United Church Press, 1994), has been very useful, as a place to start learning about Christianity, to many people.

Magazine Articles

"A Catechism for Today's Storytellers," George Fackre and Dorothy Fackre (*Youth 23:23-42,* July 1972). This looks at the basics of Christianity on a level that is appropriate for all ages.

"Denominations as Dual Structures: An Organizational Analysis," Mark Chaves (*Sociology of Religion 54(2):*147-69, 1993).

"Organizing and Sustaining Committee Life," Marliss Rogers (*Action Information 15(5)*, September-October 1989).

"Plenty Good Room: Adaptation in a Changing Black Church," Cheryl Townsend Gikes (*The Annals of the American Academy of Political and Social Science*. Vol. 558:101-121, July 1998)

Other Resources

"The Basics of Christianity," by Richard Floyd, is an unpublished course that provides a useful eight-lesson introduction to Christianity. The course covers the following questions: How do we know God? How do we interpret the Bible? What meaning do the creeds and doctrines of the church have for us today? How do we pray (the Lord's Prayer)? What is worship? What do Baptism and the Lord's Supper mean? What do the Ten Commandments tell us about our lives? What is the church?

Interfaith Message Forum (http://forums.delphi.com/ifmarriage/) is an interfaith marriage board that is very robust and filled with lots of topics and great discussion. Anyone affiliated with interfaith marriage can participate, but free registration is required.

Looking for God is a series of three videotapes from Seraphim Communications (1-800-773-3413). It is complete with a leader's guide and an excellent group of speakers. Included in the series are segments called "Looking for God in the Human Face, Form, in Nature, and in Mystery." Each segment is about twenty minutes. The set is excellent for churches that do not have a lot of time but want to cover a lot of material.